Arthur Miller's

The Crucible

Study notes for Common Module:
Texts and Human Experiences
2019–2023 HSC

Bruce Pattinson
and Lewis Mitchell

A
FIVE SENSES
PUBLICATION

Five Senses Education Pty Ltd
2/195 Prospect Highway
Seven Hills 2147
New South Wales
Australia

First Published 2018

Pattinson, Bruce and Mitchell, Lewis
Top Notes – The Crucible
ISBN 978-1-76032-217-5

CONTENTS

TOP NOTES SERIES

This series has been created to assist HSC students of English in their understanding of set texts. Top Notes are easy to read, providing analysis of issues and discussion of important ideas contained in the texts.

Particular care has been taken to ensure that students are able to examine each text in the context of the module it has been allocated to.

Each text generally includes:

- Notes on the specific module
- Plot summary
- Character analysis
- Setting
- Thematic concerns
- Language studies
- Essay questions and a modelled response
- Other textual material
- Study practice questions
- Useful quotes

We have covered the areas we feel are important for students in their study of *Text and Human Experiences* for their Common Module. I am sure you will find these Top Notes useful in your studies of English.

Bruce Pattinson
Series Editor

COMMON MODULE: TEXTS AND HUMAN EXPERIENCES

"It is quite possible—overwhelmingly probable, one might guess—that we will always learn more about human life and personality from novels than from scientific psychology"

NOAM CHOMSKY

What is the Common Module?

The Common Module set for the 2019–23 HSC is *Texts and Human Experiences*. It is compulsory to study this topic as prescribed by NESA and it is common to all three English courses. Remember: you will be learning how texts reveal individual and collective human experiences. There are no right or wrong answers in this module – it is about how you see and interpret material and engage with it.

In the Common Module you will be analysing one prescribed text and a range of short texts that are related to the idea of human experiences. You will analyse texts not only to investigate the ideas they present about this area but also how they convey these ideas. This means you will be looking closely at the techniques a composer uses to represent his / her messages and shape meaning. You will also be looking at relationships between texts in regard to the experiences you explore. Overall, you will become an expert on texts and the human experience—that is, the different notions people have about human experience and the various ways composers manipulate techniques to communicate their ideas about it.

Specifically you will look at one set text from the following list.

- Doerr, Anthony, *All the Light We Cannot See*
- Lohrey, Amanda, *Vertigo*
- Orwell, George, *Nineteen Eighty-Four*
- Parrett, Favel, *Past the Shallows*
- Dobson, Rosemary 'Young Girl at a Window', 'Over the Hill', 'Summer's End', 'The Conversation', 'Cock Crow', 'Amy Caroline', 'Canberra Morning'
- Slessor, Kenneth 'Wild Grapes', 'Gulliver', 'Out of Time', 'Vesper-Song of the Reverend Samuel Marsden', 'William Street', 'Beach Burial'
- Harrison, Jane, *Rainbow's End*
- Miller, Arthur, *The Crucible*
- Shakespeare, William, *The Merchant of Venice*
- Winton, Tim, *The Boy Behind the Curtain* Chapters: 'Havoc: A Life in Accidents', 'Betsy', 'Twice on Sundays', 'The Wait and the Flow', 'In the Shadow of the Hospital', 'The Demon Shark', 'Barefoot in the Temple of Art'
- Yousafzai, Malala & Lamb, Christina, *I am Malala*
- Daldry, Stephen, *Billy Elliot*
- O'Mahoney, Ivan, *Go Back to Where You Came From* – Series 1, Episodes 1, 2 and 3 and *The Response*
- Walker, Lucy, *Waste Land*

NESA has mandated that students must study a related text as part of the common module, and that this should be part of their in-school assessment. However there is NO LONGER a requirement to write about a related text in the HSC examination itself.

WHAT DOES NESA REQUIRE FOR THE COMMON MODULE?

The NESA documentation of the Common Module: Texts and Human Experiences states that students:

- deepen their understanding of how texts represent individual and collective human experiences;
- examine how texts represent human qualities and emotions associated with, or arising from, these experiences;
- appreciate, explore, interpret, analyse and evaluate the ways language is used to shape these representations in a range of texts in a variety of forms, modes and media;
- explore how texts may give insight into the anomalies, paradoxes and inconsistencies in human behaviour and motivations, inviting the responder to see the world differently, to challenge assumptions, ignite new ideas or reflect personally;
- may also consider the role of storytelling throughout time to express and reflect particular lives and cultures;
- by responding to a range of texts, further develop skills and confidence using various literary devices, language concepts, modes and media to formulate a considered response to texts;
- study one prescribed text and a range of short texts that provide rich opportunities to further explore representations of human experiences illuminated in texts;

- make increasingly informed judgements about how aspects of these texts, for example, context, purpose, structure, stylistic and grammatical features, and form shape meaning;
- select one related text and draw from personal experience to make connections between themselves, the world of the text and their wider world;
- by responding and composing throughout the module, further develop a repertoire of skills in comprehending, interpreting and analysing complex texts;
- examine how different modes and media use visual, verbal and/or digital language elements;
- communicate ideas using figurative language to express universal themes and evaluative language to make informed judgements about texts;
- further develop skills in using metalanguage, correct grammar and syntax to analyse language and express a personal perspective about a text

If this is what is required by NESA, we need to examine the concept of human experience carefully so we can adequately respond in these ways. I would recommend that you read the complete document which is on the NESA web site and can be downloaded in Word or Adobe. Understanding this document is an important step in handling the textual material within the guidelines required—remember you are reading for a purpose and should make notes and highlight ideas as you read so that you can develop these ideas later.

UNDERSTANDING THE COMMON MODULE

What are Human Experiences?

The concept of Human Experiences is at the heart of the Common Module.

Human Experiences are experiences of individuals or a group of people (eg a family, society, or nation) in life. There are a very wide range of human experiences which include but go beyond this list:

- feelings or reactions (momentary or long term): love, hate, anger, joy, fear, disgust
- key milestones or stages: birth, childhood, adulthood, marriage, divorce, death
- culture, belonging and identity
- conformity and rebellion
- innocence and guilt, justice
- freedom and repression
- education, vocation, work, sport, leisure
- attraction to a person, idea, group or cause
- opposition to an idea, cause, political system
- religious faith or belief
- extreme events such as an earthquake, avalanche, tsuanami
- regular events such as walking, eating, singing, dancing, discussing ideas.

The word *experience* seems innately connected to the human condition and it is something we have each day whether a mundane experience that is repetitive, or something new and dramatic which offers challenges and rewards. Experiences can vary greatly in their impact on individuals, groups and countries. One example might be a war that is a negative experience for a whole population while we may experience the wonder of medicine with a new vaccine for a deadly disease that saves millions of people. We need to note that the module asks for 'experiences' ...we are a combination of different experiences and each has a varying impact. One person's problem is another's challenge depending on perspective, skill set, previous experience and ability.

Experiences are widespread and often shared: this is why people tell their stories and these shared experiences form part of our cultural heritage. These experiences often inform, warn and teach across entire cultural groups and many stories are shared across cultures.

DEFINING HUMAN EXPERIENCES

Now let's attempt to define what human experiences are and shape them into a more coherent and easily understood framework so we can begin our investigation at a basic level of understanding before moving into more complex analysis and looking at how the texts illuminate our understanding of the term.

Dictionary.com defines the term **experience** as:

noun

1. a particular instance of personally encountering or undergoing something:
2. the process or fact of personally observing, encountering, or undergoing something:
3. the observing, encountering, or undergoing of things generally as they occur in the course of time:
   to learn from experience; the range of human experience.
4. knowledge or practical wisdom gained from what one has observed, encountered, or undergone, e.g. *a man of experience.*
5. *Philosophy.* the totality of the cognitions given by perception; all that is perceived, understood, and remembered.

verb

(used with object), **experienced, experiencing.**

6. to have experience of; meet with; undergo; feel, e.g. *to experience nausea.*
7. to learn by experience.

idiom

8. **experience religion**, to undergo a spiritual conversion by which one gains or regains faith in God.

Obviously there are a number of definitions according to context, but all are applicable to our study in some shape or form, as the range of human experience is so vast. The search for 'new experience' has driven much of the development of people, groups, cultures and nations over past millennia. New experiences are always met with excitement and often trepidation as to what change they might bring.

Think historically about how people have reacted to change. It can cause great upheavals in society, with violent reactions while other changes brought through various experiences are welcomed and may change how people live and comprehend the world. Experiences affect us emotionally in many cases rather than logically and when we respond emotionally, behaviours become unpredictable. This causes the paradoxes, anomalies and inconsistencies mentioned in the rubric. If we were logical beings the world would be an easier place, but probably more boring.

These definitions all point to the fact that memory is the key to experience. The experience is stored in memory and drawn upon when the circumstances are repeated or closely mimicked so we can deal with them — hopefully better than on the initial experience.

Experiences can come in many ways and the synonyms listed below for experience help us to understand the concept even further. They assist in defining how an experience can arise:

Synonyms

actions
background
contacts
involvement
know-how
maturity
participation
patience
practice
reality
sense
skill
struggle
training
understanding
wisdom
acquaintances
actuality
caution
combat
doings
empiricism
evidence
existences
exposures
familiarity
intimacy
inwardness
judgment
observation
perspicacity
practicality
proofs
savoir-faire
seasonings
sophistication
strife
trials
worldliness
forebearance

http://www.thesaurus.com/browse/experience?s=t

These synonyms show partly the vast array of words that our language has created around this concept, and also shows how important it is in the human psyche. We, as humans, want to experience. Now we will look at some examples of experiences and examine how they can have an impact. It is also important to remember that experiences do not have to be positive. You might experience a huge problem, a bereavement, a car accident, an unwelcome relationship or something totally bizarre that rocks your world. There can be a more opaque side to any experience that may need to be addressed.

The whole aim of this Common Module is to examine the text closely but also relate it to the concept of human experiences and decide how examining it in this way enables us to better understand both the text and the concept of humanity.

It is important that you unpack what each text you study shows you about human experiences and what ideas / themes arise from those experiences. Formulate your own ideas about the text.

Read the NESA Stage 6 document called *English Stage 6: Annotations of selected texts prescribed for the Higher School Certificate 2019–23* (see *www.educationstandards.nsw.edu.au*) for the set text you are studying. This document offers insights into the way each particular text should be examined by outlining key ideas and areas for clarification.

Human experiences and ways of experiencing vary due to individual circumstance and these experiences can change many things about individual lives, communities and the world. When we examine the concept of human experience in relation to a text, we need to examine the assumptions or biases we bring to it as well as how experiencing the text itself may change us and how we view things. The text may challenge and confront how we view the human experience or we may have preconceived ideas that make it more difficult for this to happen.

Students can also think about their own 'personal experience to make connections between themselves, the world of the text and their wider world.' Examining and enjoying any text is an experience in itself but it is what we take away from the text and apply that is the crucial aspect. That is not to say that every text will be enjoyed or offer a human experience that is significant either positively or negatively. Some texts may not personally engage you and that is fine. This is especially so when you begin to look for other related material that links to *Texts and Human Experiences*. We recommend that you find examples of texts that link but also personally appeal to you so that you can relate empathetically with them.

Individual Human Experiences

The idea of personal experiences is a popular and pervasive concept, especially in the literature of many cultures. Recording personal experiences as a means of sharing wisdom or more mundane daily tasks is part of human nature and we record and relate these experiences frequently. Experiences are recorded and relayed in many ways. We tell oral stories in both anecdotal and formal ways, we write, draw, sing and photograph our way into history (or not). Look at the proliferation of social media in this current century as people record their daily, even hourly, experiences for all to see. We record the most trivial details of our lives for likes and followers while the real world passes us by. Human experiences affect us on a daily basis and some experiences influence our lives and the way we live them.

Individuals seek out experiences in a variety of ways. Some seek more and more extreme experiences to test themselves against the world. Others limit their experiences. A lot of people prefer the familiar and don't actively seek new experiences. Individuals, it must be remembered, also see experiences in different ways and the same experience may have a very different impact on individuals. The one thing we can be certain about is that experiences are part of humanity and even the most limited of us have them. Many of these experiences also come from interaction with others and as noted we also like to share these experiences.

Experiences are what define us in many ways and are what makes us human.

We are going to look at four specific ways that experiences can influence us as people over the next few pages. These are physical, psychological, emotional and intellectual experiences and many experiences are a combination of these.

Physical Experience

The concept of a physical experience is tied into the human experience and part of the collective experience as well. Individuals seek physical experiences to test themselves against nature and other individuals often as part of trials and rituals, for example being integrated into a community. In modern times individuals have sought to test themselves with extreme sports and explorations into the harshest conditions and even space. Physical experiences can also change the way we see the world and others because of the chemical changes these experiences have on our bodies and mind. Physical experiences are often challenges and part of the experience is overcoming adversity. These physical challenges are often celebrated, as in the case of sports, but can also offer challenges if the experience is a negative one such as an accident or disease. Physical experiences are also often quite public and thus have permeated our societies in both their execution and how they are perceived. These physical experiences, even if experienced vicariously, have become popular across cultures and celebrated. Think of examples for yourself but most competitive sports offer examples.

Bruce Lee extends the concept of the physical experience into all aspects of life and that's what we will look at next in our analysis of human experiences –

> *'If you always put limits on everything you do, physical or anything else, it will spread into your work and into your life. There are no limits. There are only plateaus, and you must not stay there, you must go beyond them.'*

Psychological Experience

The idea of a psychological experience is tied into many of the abstract ideas that people experience and can lead to a discussion of what is normal psychology. From the earliest times humans have attempted to alter their psychology through a number of experiences. On a simple level this can be a drug that changes the person's or group's perspective on reality. Examples of this might be alcohol or marijuana but cultural groups also use various substances to share group experiences. This can be seen in Native American cultures with *peyote*. In more modern times prescription drugs that are mood altering have been used to minimise the symptoms of psychiatric illnesses such as depression, and these mood altering drugs are common and legal. Others attempt to alter their psychology by seeing specialists in this area while others act out their condition leading to social and criminal issues. When discussing the human experience, psychology is a key issue and will form a part of most studies of experience. When taken too far this search for a new psychological experience can be harmful eg. an addiction.

Carl Jung, the famous psychologist, comments on the problems of addiction for human experiences, stating clearly that excess can be an issue:

> *"Every form of addiction is bad, no matter whether the narcotic be alcohol, morphine or idealism."*

Emotional Experience

According to the psychologist, Robert Plutchik, there are eight basic emotions:

- **Fear** — feeling afraid.
- **Anger** — feeling angry. A stronger word for anger is rage.
- **Sadness** — feeling sad. Other words are sorrow, grief (a stronger feeling, for example when someone has died) or **depression** (feeling sad for a long time without any external cause). Some people think depression is a different emotion.
- **Joy** — feeling happy. Other words are happiness, gladness.
- **Disgust** — feeling something is wrong or nasty
- **Trust** — a positive emotion; admiration is stronger; **acceptance** is weaker
- **Anticipation** — in the sense of looking forward positively to something which is going to happen. **Expectation** is more neutral; **dread** is more negative.

https://simple.wikipedia.org/wiki/List_of_emotions

Emotions are the strongest drivers of human experience and form lasting aspects of any experience. Think about breaking up with someone you love and the emotions that drive behaviours in this situation. People have all sorts of extreme behaviours under the influence of emotions and these experiences are often the ones recorded and those which influence us most. Think about the role emotions play in our lives and the range of emotions from the list above. Consider how much emotions affect our life experiences, how they influence our decisions which decide our experiences and on a higher level consider how they affect the decisions which may seriously impact our experiences, such as politicians going to war.

Intellectual Experience

The concept of an intellectual experience is linked to decisions and experiences we have based on analysis and logic rather than the emotional choices referred to in the previous section. These intellectual experiences have changed the way we live and how we have seen our world. These experiences have affected the way we as humans have altered our world to suit our needs and lead to all the great advances in human society and thus experiences. Changes in our ideas, beliefs etc. alter the way we interact with the world and often these intellectual changes come at great cost.

Think of the time in Europe when the Church dominated and stopped scientific advances by calling them heresy/witchcraft. Open societies are more open to new ideas and this is what has hastened the pace of intellectual experiences as dominant ideologies fall away. Intellectual advances may not have the excitement that the other types produce but perhaps they have a more lasting impact on people, societies and the world in general. Ideas are powerful experiences and people hold beliefs strongly.

Immanuel Kant stated that:

> *"experience without theory is blind, but theory without experience is mere intellectual play."*

Consider this statement in the light of what we have learnt about human experiences. Are they a combination of many factors or can we isolate experiences into simple forms?

What exactly is a human experience?

The titular question reminds us of the old brainteaser: "If a tree falls in a forest and no one is around to hear it, does it make a sound?"

There are two classic responses to this. The more Platonically-minded would say the tree always makes a sound when it falls in the forest. We don't have to be there to hear it; we can imagine the sound of a tree falling in the forest, based on memory of such an event or on the recording of such an event. We know that sound is just vibrating air, and it's safe to say that air always vibrates in response to a tree falling, or a bear growling, or a cicada singing, whether we are there to hear it or not.

The second answer is a more post-structuralist response: the sound doesn't occur on its own; it needs a human ear to be heard. Therefore, if there is no human in the forest to hear the tree fall, then there is no sound. This automatically implies that "experience" of anything requires the presence of a human being, which means there is no such thing as an experience that *isn't* human.

Animal rights activists – or anyone with a beloved pet – would almost certainly reject this notion because it prioritises humans and relegates all other species to a lower class of being: an attitude that most would agree has gotten the human race into an awful lot of environmental trouble over the last 200 years of industrialisation.

In his article (*What is an Experience?*), my learned colleague Paul Hartley describes experience in its most basic form, as "the perception of something else" and "ultimately information about what we have perceived." But does this make it particularly human? Dogs and cats perceive things. Insects perceive things. You could even say that plants perceive things, such as the direction from which the sun is shining. Perception is the most basic of life's survival tools for all manner of flora and fauna.

In her brief but cogent disquisition on the subject (*What is Human?*), another of my learned colleagues, Nadine Hare, asserts that to be human is a social construct. Hartley builds on that notion by suggesting that culture affects experience when we start to share it, because "the words, associations, and priorities we attach to the shared experience define how we understand the world we live in."

Hare rightly points out that this world is increasingly dominated by consumerism, which has distorted what it means to be human by excluding all of the attributes and qualities that "make people people." Calling us consumers reduces our experiences to mere transactions. It defines human experience within the narrow confines of the purchase funnel and has little interest in anything that isn't a purchase driver.

Perhaps the field of commerce is where the experiential rubber most emphatically meets the road. Unlike mere perception, commerce is a uniquely human experience. It has mediated, automated, and dominated the human agenda to the point where we are defined by what we buy and little else. Commerce has invaded the non-profit spheres of government, health, and education, imposing its own priorities and principles on these institutions in the expectation that they will behave more like businesses. And even though business still strives to appeal to the so-called masses, it prioritises the pursuit of individual wealth, and in so doing, not only inhibits the desire for shared experience but unravels the social fabric historically woven by the democratic tradition.

As if in response, that social fabric is being re-woven by our networks. As Hare asserts, "humans both produce technology and are produced through technology." Experience is shared more now than it ever has been because the experiential platform – i.e., that very human invention called the internet – is in place to facilitate it like never before, and on a global scale.

This sharing capability reintroduces all of those things that "make people people" back into the conversation – whether commercial or political. What "makes people people" is messy, unpredictable, emotional, and complex. Most of what makes us human has no place in the experiential confines of the purchase funnel, and defies any of our attempts to place it there.

The challenge for us as a species is to embrace this new capacity for sharing to keep the agendas of our hegemonic institutions – whether commercial or political – from defining what makes an experience human. A post-consumer business strategy might be one that, as Hare hopes, will "expand our view of people to include the complex and dynamic social, cultural, gendered, spiritual and racialised beings that they are." Maybe then will our shared human experience truly become, as Hartley asserts, the glue that holds us all together as human beings.

Will Novosedlik
MISC magazine
https://miscmagazine.com/what-is-a-human-experience/

This article appeared in the September 2014 edition of MISC magazine. Can you relate to what the article says about human experiences? Do human experiences depend on perception? Does the experience of anything require the presence of a human as experiencer (para 3)? Can the ideas of experience be extended to include perception by plants or animals? Hartley's idea is that "shared human experience" is "the glue that holds us all together as human beings". Is this an oversimplification?

The Impact of Human Experiences

Human experiences have impacts on many levels. On an individual level, we can have changes in our assumptions about the world and people around us; we can ingest new ideas and have these open new vistas of productivity and performance. We can also reflect and build on these experiences to ensure that they are even more meaningful to our lives. Behaviours towards others and the way we respond to the world can manifest themselves in new and different responses. An example might be that through adverse experiences we can build resilience so that the next negative experience isn't as traumatic and we accept it for what it is. Experiences also teach us new behaviours on a very physical level—if you burn yourself once on a flame you learn not to do it again (hopefully).

The impact of human experiences can also be shared in groups and societies. Firstly, let's examine some group dynamics that can be affected by human experiences. Groups share experiences and adapt and develop behaviours that impact on the group as a whole. Think about the notorious 'bonding' sessions sporting teams have that unite them in a common goal. Think about the behaviours of various gangs in our society. We see plenty of examples of this on American television where gangs based on ethnicity and social groupings form specific sets of behaviours that impact on how they interact with each other and the world. These groupings carry assumptions about how they see the world and respond to it. For example, they may have generally negative reactions to law enforcement and this is ingrained into their codes of behaviour. They are suspicious of the world and the people in it—dividing them up into threats, the law and victims. These behaviours are often reinforced by group experiences such as the initiation rituals which are integral to membership.

Often the impact of these behaviours is to perpetuate stereotypes that then categorise the individuals within these groups. The graphic I have included here shows a stereotypical gang member with the suspicious gaze, ubiquitous hoody and scruffy look. These stereotypes reject new ideas and maintain assumptions about the world, often to the detriment of their members. The experiences they have reinforce their own stereotypical way of viewing anything outside the safety of the group and the cycle continues. Of course, other groups have more positive impacts and see the world as a very different place and their experiences are designed to be positive interactions. Think about groups such as Rotary who are constructive in the community. Other groups have specialty interests such as Animal Welfare, Surf Lifesaving and charities.

Normal social interactions impact groups and individuals, but it takes a major event to alter the behaviours of whole societies, especially so in the modern world where societies are large in scale. Earlier in human history smaller experiences could alter the behaviour of societies as they were insignificant in size compared to modern ones. We often fail to remember that many of these ancient societies' behaviours were impacted by superstition, religions and cultural habituation. The modern society as we know it is only a recent phenomenon. Just a few hundred years ago with church rule people were forced to think in a specific

way and punished for not adhering to a theological culture. Think of the Spanish Inquisition, the imprisonment of Galileo and other such restrictions on freedom of thought; scientific breakthroughs were hidden or declared witchcraft. Even recently the world has seen societies kept repressed by failed ideologies. The brutality of such regimes has left deep scars on the social psyche of nations as they try to recover. This has had an impact on the human experiences of whole populations, and societies respond accordingly.

One example might be at the conclusion of the Communist regime in East Germany when the Berlin Wall was destroyed as a visual symbol of the new-found freedom of a whole population of people who had been repressed for decades by a brutal and ever-present regime. Many citizens who had grown up in this system, where you could 'disappear' without trial or real evidence, found the idea that you could express yourself incredible. Many of the

East Germans couldn't believe that this freedom was real and that the Stasi (the secret police) were gone.

Other experiences can affect societies in extreme ways. Think about wars and the impact they have on civilian populations.

Climatic events such as earthquakes change the way that people behave and respond to situations. Catastrophic flooding occurred in the US city of New Orleans in 2005. The US President's response to help was not immediate and the national administration was severely criticised for lack of effective action.

Societies also respond to perceived problems such as pollution. In 1989 the oil tanker Exxon Valdez ran aground in Prince William Sound, Alaska with disastrous results. The effects of this event are still being experienced thirty years later.

Societies can be divided, as we saw with the election of Donald Trump in the United States of America and the reaction of the Political Left.

The impact of human experiences on societies can be quite dramatic, as we have seen, while other experiences (such as an election) can go by without a murmur from societies, no matter who wins. As a last thought before we move on you should also consider the impact of the media on societies in the modern world, and how they influence individuals, societies and the development of ideas.

Problems With Human Behaviour

So far, we have discussed the impact of human experiences on behaviour. Now we can begin to develop some more complex judgements and understandings about the impact of those experiences on human behaviours. In simplistic terms it could be assessed as:

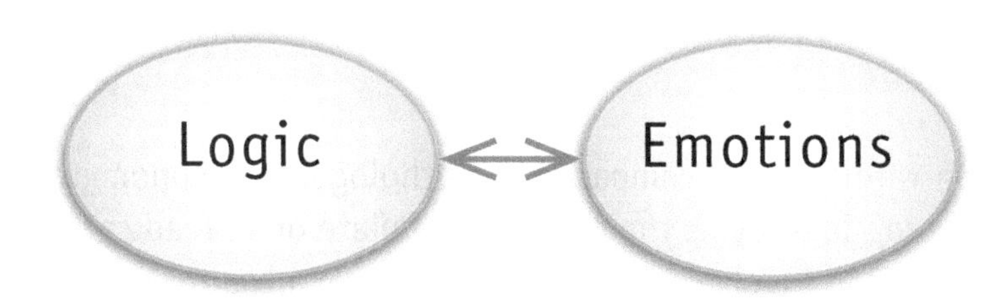

These two opposites on the continuum certainly shape the manner in which we see incidents and how they affect the experience. For instance, if someone you love has no interest in you, it creates a very different reaction to someone you don't care about having no interest in you. It is generally agreed that humans respond more strongly with emotion than they do with logic. Often, it is only through time and reflection that we can understand how an experience has changed and/or altered the manner in which we see a situation or individual.

The Role of Storytelling in Human Experiences

Storytelling has been part of the human experience since 'people' began communicating and it is a method used to convey information and experience as well as be entertaining. Earliest myths were all oral and then people began to write down stories so they weren't lost in time. From this, various theories have developed around storytelling and one is the 'monomyth', which is a template across cultures for storytelling. Let's have a look at this below.

'In narratology and comparative mythology, the monomyth, or the hero's journey, is the common template of a broad category of tales that involve a hero who goes on an adventure, and in a decisive crisis wins a victory, and then comes home changed or transformed.

The concept was introduced in *The Hero with a Thousand Faces* (1949) by Joseph Campbell, who described the basic narrative pattern as follows:

> "A hero ventures forth from the world of common day into a region of supernatural wonder: fabulous forces are there encountered and a decisive victory is won: the hero comes back from this mysterious adventure with the power to bestow boons on his fellow man."

Campbell and other scholars, such as Erich Neumann, describe narratives of Gautama Buddha, Moses, and Christ in terms of the monomyth. Critics argue that the concept is too broad or general to be of much use in comparative mythology. Others say that the hero's journey is only a part of the monomyth; the other part is a sort of different form, or colour, of the hero's journey.

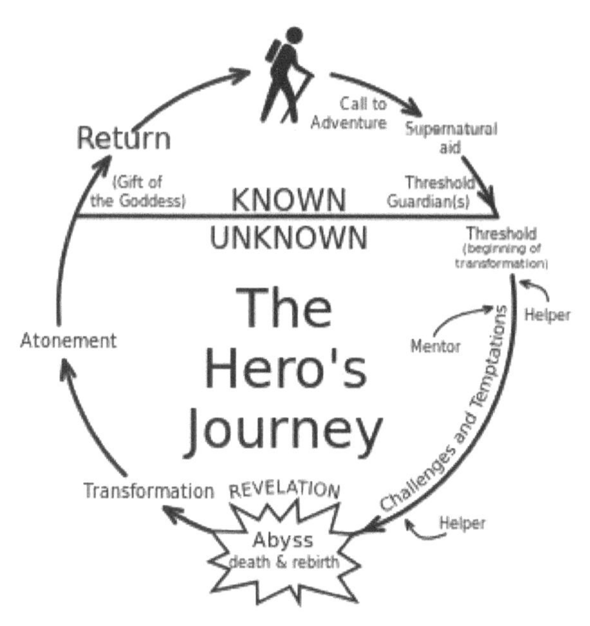

https://en.wikipedia.org/wiki/Hero%27s_journey

Storytelling in History and its Purpose in Human Experience

Storytelling in oral form was accompanied by some theatrics to make the stories as entertaining as possible. Many of the early narratives were based upon religious ceremonies and stories of the creation of the earth and people(s). As time moved on, these stories were accompanied by dance, music and / or theatre and often were part of lengthy rituals, often taking days. These stories were designed to bring meaning to people's lives by explaining their own existence and the purpose / meaning of life in a time when life expectancy was short and entertainment was scarce. Of course stories were also recorded as these experiences were significant to all people and these stories run across all cultures. Before writing, stories were recorded in pictures such as cave art, in tattoo designs on skin and in designs such as rock piles and the giant carved heads of Easter Island.

Writing changed the manner in which stories were told and many of the old oral traditions were lost, barely being kept alive by specialists. Stories began to travel across cultural and national boundaries on whatever surface could be created. Papyrus, bones, pottery, skins, paper and in more modern times film, video and digital storage have changed, over time, the way in which stories of human experience have been told and shared. Content evolved from myth, fable and legend to history, personal narratives and commentary. Modern narrative form often has an educational or didactic element and can drift into propaganda. Stories of self-revelation can be instructive and give audiences the opportunity to apply learning to individual lives, whereas historically narrative was used in this way for societies and groups as a whole. In recent times narratives have become interactive and audiences can choose how the narrative unfolds.

Whatever form the story takes we all have a seemingly innate need for narratives to make sense of our lives. They either confirm our world view or alter our world view depending on the experience they convey and the experiences that we bring to the narrative. We need to remember that narratives are important to human experience and have been significant since the beginning of time.

The Text as an Experience

The concept of the text as an experience is one area to consider as we look at *Texts and Human Experiences*. Reading or viewing the text is an experience in itself and when we do this we bring our own history (experiences) to the text and this helps shape our understanding.

Think about the personal perspective that you bring to a text. What are some of your experiences that might influence how you read a particular text? Some texts, especially personal narratives of trial and tribulation or loss, can be confronting to some audiences and bring back strong opinions or emotions. Many texts attempt to do this as they convey a particular point of view about the world.

Does what you bring to the text affect what you learn from that text? We also need to delve into how the narrative experience is conveyed and how this in turn impacts upon the manner in which the story is received by audiences across different cultures. For example, Western films where heroes fight Islamic terrorism may well be viewed very differently by audiences in Western democracies and Islamic countries. Even seemingly innocuous narratives like the movie 'The Red Pill' which is about men's rights and created by a woman, has caused a polarisation of views wherever it has been shown. Strong personal experiences and viewpoints certainly bring their own understandings to texts.

Questions for Texts and Human Experiences

- Define the module in your own words.
- How are people connected by shared experiences?
- How might physical experience(s) change the way you respond to the world?
- How do you think a person's context and prior experiences shape how they perceive the world?
- Are experiences unique or do prior experiences have an impact on a current experience and way of seeing life?
- What is positive about human experiences?
- Discuss what is negative about human experiences.
- To what extent does experience shape the way we see other people and / or groups?
- Is an individual's culture part of their experience or is it something else?
- Is it possible not to have any meaningful experiences at all?
- Why do people tell stories?
- What do you think you might learn from a narrative?

STUDYING A DRAMA TEXT

The medium of any text is very important. If a text is a drama this must not be forgotten. Plays are not *read* they are *viewed*. This means you should never refer to the "reader" but the "audience" as the respondent to the text.

The marker will want to know you are aware of the text as a play and that you have considered its effect in performance.

Remembering a drama text is a play also means when you are exploring *how* the composer represents his / her ideas you MUST discuss dramatic techniques. This applies to any response you do using a drama, irrespective of the form the response is required to be in.

Dramatic techniques are all the devices the playwright uses to represent his or her ideas. They are the elements of a drama that are manipulated by playwrights and directors to make any drama effective on stage! You might also see them referred to as dramatic devices or theatrical techniques.

Every play uses dramatic techniques differently. Some playwrights are very specific about how they want their play performed on stage. Others like Shakespeare give virtually no directions. They might give detailed comments at the beginning of the play and / or during the script. These are usually in italics and are called *stage directions*. They are never spoken but provide a guide to the director and actors about how the play is to appear and sound when performed.

Some common dramatic techniques are shown on the diagram that follows.

DRAMATIC TECHNIQUES

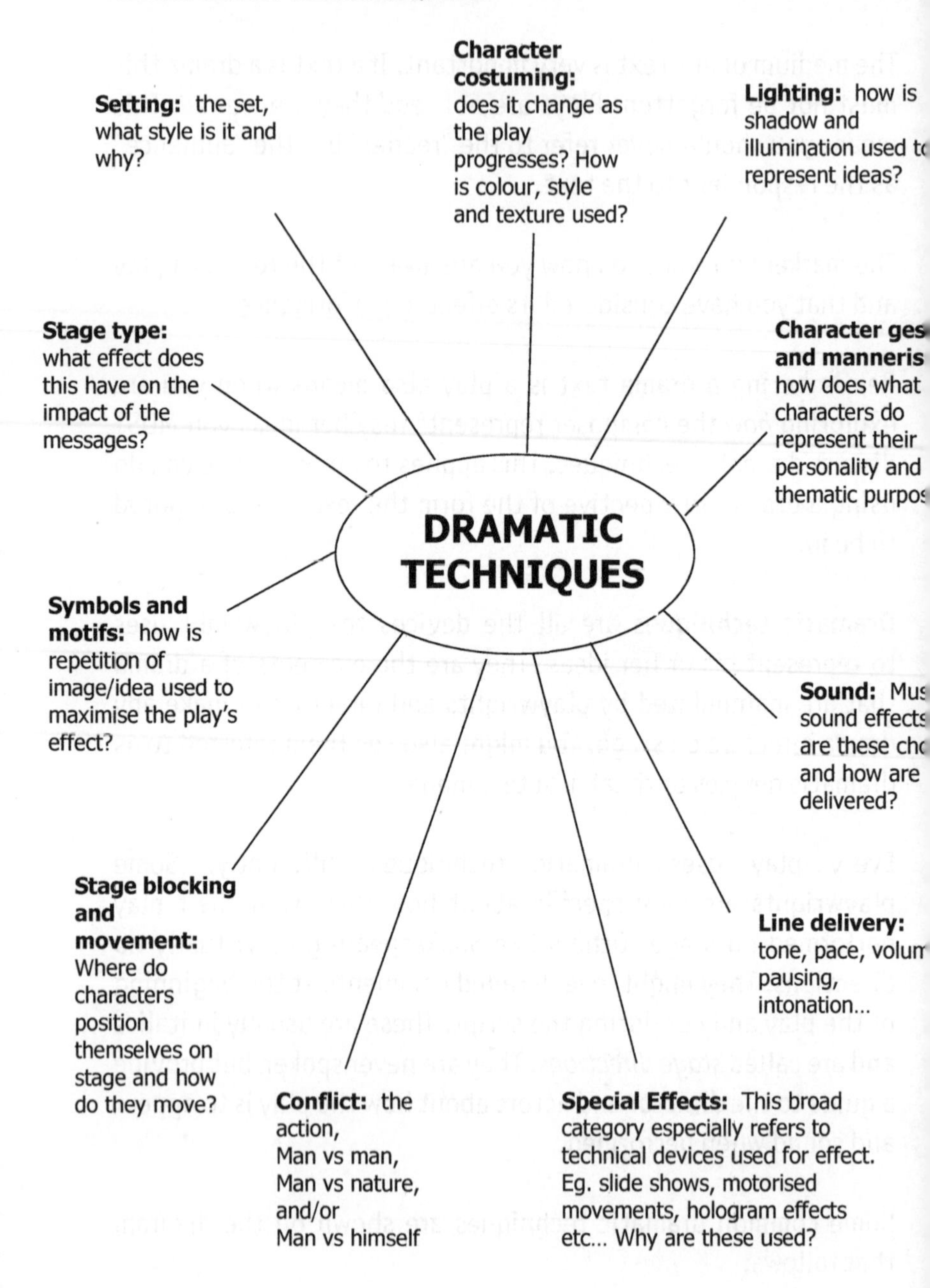

DRAMATIC TECHNIQUES
Character costuming: does it change as the play progresses? How is colour, style and texture used?
Setting: the set, what style is it and why?
Lighting: how is shadow and illumination used t
represent ideas?
Stage type: what effect does this have on the impact of the messages?
Character ges
and manneris
how does what characters do represent their personality and thematic purpo
Symbols and motifs: how is repetition of image/idea used to maximise the play's effect?
Sound: Mu
sound effect
are these ch
and how are delivered?
Stage blocking and movement: Where do characters position themselves on stage and how do they move?
Line delivery: tone, pace, volu
pausing, intonation...
Conflict: the action, Man vs man, Man vs nature, and/or Man vs himself
Special Effects: This broad category especially refers to technical devices used for effect. Eg. slide shows, motorised movements, hologram effects etc... Why are these used?

THE PLAYWRIGHT – ARTHUR MILLER

Born in New York City in 1915 to middle-class Jewish parents, Arthur Miller went on to become one of the most important American dramatists of the 20th century. His 1949 play *Death of a Salesman* is a seminal work of the American theatre, representing the origins and impact of what is often called 'The American Dream'.

The Crucible was first performed in 1953. In it, Miller examines the issues surrounding the contemporary actions of Senator Joseph McCarthy, and his attempt to wipe out Communism in America, by comparing them to the famous Salem witch hunt of the 1690s. Miller was himself implicated in the McCarthy investigation into 'Un-American Activities.' The play has had a profound affect on the assessment of the McCarthy era of American politics.

His screenplays include *The Misfits* (which starred his then wife Marilyn Monroe) and *The Crucible* (1996) which was nominated for an Academy Award.

In 1956 he married Marilyn Monroe. They divorced in 1961, about a year before she died. His play *After The Fall* is about their relationship.

His autobiography, *Time Bends*, was published in 1987. Arthur Miller died in 2005.

CONTEXT

McCarthyism in the 1950s

During the period of the late 1940s to the late 1950s, Americans became concerned about the perceived influence of Communists and possible infiltration of American institutions by Communists.

The background to this is the historical period immediately after World War II, known as The Cold War. America and Russia (The Soviet Union) emerged from World War II as the great superpowers. The expression 'The Cold War' refers to the fact that there was constant tension and distrust between the two countries, although war never actually broke out. The Soviet Union was a Communist country, meaning that the country was being run according to the principles of Communism. Americans became concerned that Communists might infiltrate American institutions and gradually take over – turning America from a Democracy into a Communist country.

From 1950 to 1954, US Senator Joseph McCarthy ran a campaign aimed at removing Communists from 'places of influence' in American society. His House Un-American Activities Committee conducted investigations into individuals, their beliefs and associates. During his time he removed thousands of people from their jobs, ruined reputations and saw that countless others lived in fear. He particularly targeted artists, theatre practitioners and the film industry.

Arthur Miller himself appeared before the committee. He refused to name the names of his associates and was convicted of 'Contempt of Congress' in May 1957. He was fined $500 and sentenced to 30 days gaol. This was overturned on appeal in 1958.

Salem Witch Hunts 1692

By the second half of the 17th century, the Puritan settlement in Plymouth New England had become a theocracy. This is a situation where church and state are bound together. Religious law becomes state law. In these circumstances, the rules normally associated with evidence in a trial can become quite distorted.

In Salem Massachusetts in 1692, a group of apparently innocent girls began identifying members of the community as having come to them as witches or cast spells upon them. Once the court believed that they were genuine, it was very difficult for the accused to defend themselves. The only way to avoid the death penalty was to admit to being in association with the devil. Many people, now regarded as totally innocent, were hanged as witches.

Arthur Miller clearly identified similarities between McCarthyism and the Salem Witch Trials. In each, a society, operating on the basis of fear, overreacts to some kind of threat by denying individuals their normal rights. People were rewarded for naming others as suspects and those accused could only avoid conviction by confessing. In these circumstances, justice became impossible and the rule of fear prevails. Miller wrote a play about Salem 1692 that reflected on America in 1953.

You might accuse Miller of being too frightened or timid to write a play that was directly about McCarthy and the Communist investigations of the 1950s. To do so would have been career suicide at the time. Also, by using the Salem witch hunts and trials as a point of reference, he was better able to reflect negatively on McCarthyism. By 1953, the Salem witch trials were a famous example of superstitious hysteria resulting in terrible instances of injustice. By having his audience see similarities between McCarthy and the judges in Salem, he was able to suggest to his audience that McCarthyism would result in the same level of hysteria and injustice. He was right; McCarthy and McCarthyism had been discredited by the end of the 1950s. Today, we might see the play as reflecting on our treatment of people accused of something that is feared by society.

The Crucible is quite historically accurate. The characters all existed and their fates were as in the play. Miller, though, made a significant change in the ages of John Proctor (who was in his 60s) and Abigail Williams (who was really just 11). There is no historical evidence that they were 'involved' in the way that they are in the play.

As you can see there are some quite dramatic events that had an immense impact on many human experiences that are behind the crafting of this play. Miller develops a set of ideas in the play that reflect these experiences. It is relevant to consider the concept that historical experiences can affect the manner in which we make assumptions and generalisations about the present.

THE CRUCIBLE – PLOT OUTLINE

Betty Parris is sick and her father Reverend Parris prays for her.

Betty, with Abigail and others have been caught dancing in the woods.

The town is talking witchcraft so Parris calls for Reverend Hale of Beverley, an expert.

Abigail tells Proctor that it was just 'sport' and that she still wants him.

Abigail and the other girls accuse Tituba of conjuring spirits.

They accuse Sarah Good, Goody Osburn and others of being witches.

The Proctors speak awkwardly about Abigail.

Hale arrives and quizzes them about their faith.

Elizabeth is arrested by Cheever.

Proctor determines to go to the court and discredit Abigail.

Deputy Governor Danforth hears Mary Warren's attempt to change her evidence.

Proctor is forced to admit to having 'known' Abigail.

Elizabeth denies this, thinking she is saving him, then Mary Warren turns on him as 'the devil's man'.

In Act 4, Hale attempts to convince the prisoners to sign (false) confessions so they don't hang.

Danforth lets Elizabeth speak to Proctor to sway him to confess, but he does not. He goes to his death with goodness.

THE CRUCIBLE – PLOT SUMMARY

ACT 1

Salem, Massachusetts in the spring of 1692. The scene is an upper bedroom of the house of Reverend Samuel Parris. Reverend Parris is kneeling at the bed of his ten year old daughter Betty, praying. She does not move.

His Negro slave Tituba enters, concerned about Betty, but Parris tells her to get out. His 17 year-old orphan niece, Abigail, enters. The stage direction says she is 'strikingly beautiful' and that she has 'an endless capacity for dissembling'. The word 'dissembling' suggests that she is dishonest and manipulative, that she is capable of pretending in order to have a certain effect on others.

IMPORTANT NOTE: Remember that audiences don't read stage directions. Miller, in the text, tells us a very significant character trait of Abigail's here. It may well be a long (or at least a little) way into the play before the audience realises this.

Abigail introduces Susanna Walcott, who says that Doctor Griggs can find 'no medicine for it' (what is ailing Betty) and that Reverend Parris should consider the possibility of 'unnatural' causes. This makes Parris even more anxious. Parris is frightened that witchcraft might be involved. He says that he has called for Reverend Hale of Beverley (an expert in witchcraft) to come.

He and Abigail discuss what he saw a group of them doing in the woods. She admits to dancing, but says that Betty is not 'witched'. She says that it was just 'sport' (fun). Parris says that he thought he saw someone naked, running through the trees. He asks Abigail about her reputation in the community and she says that it is good, but that 'Goody' (Goodwife) Proctor hates her and sacked her because she wouldn't be her slave.

Parris is concerned that this scandal could bring him down. He says that there is already a faction in the church who want to get rid if him.

Mr Thomas and Mrs Ann Putnam enter, she talking about the devil and about how she heard that Betty had flown. The Putnams are middle-aged landowners, influential in the church. Mrs Putnam has had seven of her children die in infancy and she believes it is the work of a witch. She tells Parris that Tituba can speak to the dead and that she was trying to make contact with the Putnam's dead babies in order to find out who had killed them. Their only living child, Ruth was helping. Abigail is seen by Parris to have lied to him. She says that Tituba and Ruth conjured spirits, but not she. The news that a member of his own household (Tituba) was conjuring spirits sends Parris into another bout of fear about the likelihood of keeping his job. Parris goes downstairs to speak to the people who have gathered there. The Putnams go with him.

Abigail, Mercy Lewis (the Putnam's servant) and Mary Warren (the Proctor's servant) are left alone with Betty Parris. Abigail tells Mercy that 'they' know that Tituba conjured spirits, that they danced and that Parris saw Mercy naked. Mary Warren says that the town is calling them witches. Suddenly Betty rises and runs across the room, as if in fear of Abigail. She says that Abigail drank a charm to kill Goody Proctor! Abigail strikes her across the face and tells them all that they are to say that they danced and that Tituba conjured the dead Putnam babies, and that is all. She threatens them all with violent retribution should they tell of any of the other things.

John Proctor enters, ordering Mary Warren home. Mercy Lewis goes as well. 'What's this mischief here?' Proctor asks Abigail, indicating that he does not believe that it is witchcraft and he suspects that Abigail is behind it. What follows is a scene of awkward intimacy, where we learn that Proctor and Abigail have had an affair, resulting in Elizabeth (Goody) Proctor sacking Abigail from her job with them. Abigail tries to rekindle the relationship but Proctor will not have it.

As the psalm being sung down stairs rises to its climax, Betty begins to scream. Parris and the Putnams return, Ann saying that Betty cannot bear to hear the Lord's name (because she is possessed by the devil). Rebecca Nurse, who is 72, enters, and Giles Corey (who is 80). Rebecca goes to Betty and stands beside her as she gradually quietens. Rebecca describes what is happening to Betty as 'silly seasons', and she advises against looking for supernatural causes.

Discussion ensues about Parris' preaching style and his claiming of an allowance for wood, and disputes between Proctor and Putnam over land boundaries. Proctor quips that if there is an anti-Parris faction in the church then he must find it and join it. Giles and he are obviously like-minded.

Reverend Hale of Beverley enters, carrying many books 'weighted with authority'. Eventually Proctor and Rebecca go. Giles Corey asks Hale if the fact that his wife reads a lot signifies anything.

Hale interviews Abigail, who maintains her innocence of anything but dancing, but eventually turns it all onto Tituba, saying that 'she makes me drink blood.' This turns Hale's attention to Tituba who becomes increasingly hysterical, finally confessing that the Devil had come to her with Sarah (Goody) Good and Goody Osburn.

At the height of this revelation, Abigail rises and 'confesses' to having seen the Devil with Sarah Good, Goody Osburn, Bridget Bishop and George Jacobs. Suddenly Betty joins the chant, naming Martha Bellows and Alice Barrow. Hale interprets all of this as the release of the girls' spirits from the control of the devil.

Act 1 ends, as the naming continues, 'on their ecstatic cries.'

Act 2

The common room of Proctor's house, eight days later.

Elizabeth can be heard upstairs, singing to the children. Proctor enters and goes to the pot in the fireplace. He tastes the contents and adds some salt.

Later he compliments Elizabeth, saying that the stew is 'well seasoned'. This is one of many aspects of the conversation between them that indicates that things are not quite right.

She tells him that Mary Warren has been in the court all day and that things seem to be getting out of hand. She says that he should go to the court and tell them the truth, as told him by Abigail, that it was mere 'sport'. He tells her that he has no one to corroborate his story. This makes her start as he had not told her that he was alone with Abigail. She also suggests that he is trying to protect Abigail by not testifying. He says: 'Spare me!

You forget nothin' and forgive nothing.' Now the truth of their feelings is coming out.

Elizabeth says that John is judging himself: 'The magistrate sits in your heart that judges you.' She adds that she always believed he was a good man, just 'bewildered'.

Mary Warren enters, coming from the court. She gives Elizabeth a 'poppet' (a small doll made of fabric) that she has made during the day in court. She tells them that there are now 39 people arrested, that Goody Osburn will hang, but not Sarah Good because she has confessed.

Mary then discusses the sensations she has experienced in the court. She says that Sarah Good choked her and the others in the court and that Sarah had many times tried to kill her. She says that she heard screaming and then she realised it was herself. She says that the Devil is 'loose' in Salem.

The tension rises as she tells the Proctors that Elizabeth was 'somewhat mentioned' but that she put in a good word for her. Mary demands that she be treated with respect from here on, as an official of the court.

Mary goes to bed. Elizabeth predicts that Abigail will accuse her. 'She wants me dead. I knew all week it would come to this.' She asks John to go to Abigail and tell her that he will never marry her, even if Elizabeth were dead. Elizabeth is thinking to remove Abigail's motive for accusing her, but John and the audience know that he has already had this conversation with Abigail, to no avail.

Proctor's line: 'Were I stone I would have cracked for shame this seven month' is an expression of his guilt and internal conflict.

Suddenly, Mr Hale appears in the doorway. He tells them that both Rebecca Nurse and Elizabeth have been mentioned in court and that he is here to test the Christian character of the house. He begins by asking Proctor why he so rarely goes to church. Eventually Proctor admits that he 'sees no light of God' in Parris, but Hale says that as he is ordained 'the light of God' is in him. Proctor says that their last child hasn't been baptised because he didn't want Parris to touch him. Hale asks Proctor to recite the Ten Commandments and Proctor, rather uncertainly, gets to nine. Elizabeth adds 'Thou shalt not commit adultery' as the one he can't remember. Of course, Miller wants this to be seen as evidence of Proctor's repression of his sin.

Hale says the famous line: 'Theology, sir, is a fortress; no crack in a fortress may be accounted small.'

At Elizabeth's encouragement, Proctor tells Hale that Abigail had told him that it 'had naught to do with witchcraft.'

Suddenly Francis Nurse and Giles Corey arrive with the news that their wives have been arrested, Rebecca for the murder of the Putnam babies. Hale tells Francis that 'the court will send her home.' He remains sure that the devil is alive in Salem.

Next, Ezekiel Cheever and Marshal Herrick arrive to arrest Elizabeth. He takes down the poppet and discovers a needle stuck into it. He says that over dinner Abigail had fallen wailing and Parris had discovered a needle stuck in her belly. Abigail said that Elizabeth's spirit had done it.

Hale reassures them that if she is innocent it will be all right. This sets Proctor off as he asks why no one asks if Parris or Abigail is innocent. He says that 'vengeance is walking Salem' and the children are in charge.

Cheever takes Elizabeth away, as both Corey and Proctor accuse Hale of hypocrisy. It is clear that Hale is shaken by the events.

Proctor tells Mary Warren to testify that she stuck the needle into the poppet and gave it to Elizabeth, but Mary says she is too frightened of Abigail to do so. He hurls her to the floor, where she repeats: 'I cannot, I cannot...' Proctor knows he must go to the court and confess his 'knowledge' of Abigail. He says: 'we are only what we always were, but naked now.'

Act 3

The vestry room of the Salem meeting house. The meeting house is now serving as a court and the smaller vestry as an 'ante-room' of the court.

We can hear the voices coming from the court. Judge Hathorn is cross-examining Martha Corey. Giles Corey calls out 'Thomas Putnam is reaching out for land!' The door of the vestry opens and Giles is carried in by Marshal Herrick. Judge Hathorn follows him, then Deputy Governor Danforth with Cheever and Parris. Hale and Francis Nurse are also present.

Danforth tells Giles that only his old age is keeping him out of gaol for disrupting the court. Giles cries, saying that it is his own fault his wife is charged. He goes, then Francis Nurse tells Danforth that he has evidence that the girls are frauds. Danforth tells Francis about what an important and powerful judge he is. Giles re-enters with Proctor and Mary Warren.

Mary tells Danforth that the whole thing with the girls is 'pretence'. Danforth responds with the famous metaphor upon which the title of the play is based: 'We burn a hot fire here, it melts down all concealment.' This turns out to be truer than Danforth really understands, and it applies to him as well as everyone else.

Danforth turns on Proctor, asking him if he has ever seen the devil. Danforth is concerned to hear about Proctor's poor church-going record and that he tore up the warrant for Elizabeth's arrest. He tells Proctor that it has been discovered that Elizabeth is pregnant, and that will save her from execution for a year. He offers him this 'out', but Proctor looks at his friends Giles and Francis and says that he wants to proceed with his evidence.

Proctor produces a statement in support of Martha, Rebecca and Elizabeth, signed by ninety-one farmers and members of the church. Danforth, at Parris' insistence, has Herrick draw up warrants for the arrest for examination of all signatories. Francis is horrified. Hale asks: 'Is every defence an attack on the court?' Danforth responds that one is either for the court or against it, no mid-way. Danforth: 'But you must understand, sir, that a person is either with this court or he must be counted against it, there be no road between.'

Giles accuses Putnam of having his daughter call out George Jacobs in order that he would forfeit his land and Putnam could get it. He says that an honest man told him, but he refuses to give Danforth the name of the man. Danforth charges Giles with contempt of court.

Proctor gives Danforth Mary's sworn deposition that she did not see the devil or any spirits and that the girls are lying. Hale begs Danforth to have Proctor get legal representation, but Danforth sees no purpose in this. He explains that because witchcraft is an invisible crime, only the witch and the victim can be witness to it. The witch won't accuse herself, so we have to rely on the victims, and 'they do testify.' This long speech, on page 90, goes a long way to explaining the hopeless legal situation that Proctor and Giles are in – if the girls call them devil-worshippers they are put in the position where they have to try to prove they are not.

He tells Mary Warren that she is either lying now or she was lying in court, and either way she will go to gaol. He calls the girls into the vestry. Abigail denies Mary's story. Proctor tells Danforth of the dancing in the woods and he is horrified. Parris lies, saying that he didn't see anyone naked, but that they were dancing.

Hathorn demands that Mary pretend to see spirits now, but she cannot. Danforth presses Abigail, but she turns on him and warns him that even he could be tainted by the devil. Then she looks upward in fear, complaining of a cold wind. The other girls join her in this 'experience'.

Suddenly Proctor snaps and leaps at Abigail, pulling her down by the hair, saying: 'How do you call heaven! Whore! Whore!' He admits to having 'known her' and that it is her intention to 'dance with me on my wife's grave!'

Abigail steps up to Danforth, warning him: 'What look do you give me?' and 'I'll not have such looks!' Danforth cannot speak. Then he calls for Elizabeth Proctor to be brought into the room. He asks her if her husband is a lecher. At first she tries to avoid the question, but finally she lies, she thinks to save John. He cries out: 'Elizabeth, I have confessed it!'

Hale, who has been losing confidence in proceedings for some time says: 'it is a natural lie to tell', 'private vengeance is working through this testimony' and ' This girl (Abigail) has always struck me false.'

Suddenly, Abigail turns her face to the ceiling, talking to a 'bird', which 'becomes' Mary. Abigail: 'Oh, Mary, this is a black art to change your shape...It's God's work I do.'

The other girls follow her. Proctor declares it pretence, as does Mary, but the girls repeat Mary's words in unison, putting pressure onto her until she cracks and starts to scream and denounce Proctor as the devil's man. Abigail puts her arms around Mary as Danforth calls upon Proctor to confess. Proctor says that 'we will burn together' and 'you know in your black hearts that this be fraud.'

Hale says: 'I denounce these proceedings, I quit this court.'

ACT 4

The scene is a cell in the Salem Jail. A few months have passed. Tituba and Sarah Good are together in the cell. Tituba is talking dreamily about returning to Barbados.

Hathorn and Danforth arrive. Hathorn says that Parris has a mad look lately, indicating some kind of change in him. Parris arrives, with the news that Abigail has stolen 31 pounds from him and disappeared along with Mercy Lewis. He also says that Hale spends his time trying to convince the prisoners to confess and be allowed to live. Later, Hale describes himself as doing the devil's work in counselling Christians to sign their names to lies (false confessions). He is a broken man: 'Can you not see the blood on my head!!'

Parris fears rebellion if Rebecca Nurse is hanged. 'Judge Hathorn – it were another sort that hanged till now.' He means that Rebecca has a high degree of respect in the community and that people will react to her hanging in a way that they did not to the hanging of the others. The truth is that no-one believes that Rebecca Nurse could possibly have consorted with the devil. Danforth's response is more to do with maintaining the power of the court rather than having it actually dispense justice. Danforth declares that there will be no postponement of the hangings, saying 'Postponement speaks a floundering on my part.' This is a response based on maintaining Danforth's ego rather than dispensing justice.

Danforth calls for Elizabeth Proctor in the hopes that she can talk Proctor into confessing. Proctor is led in, bearded and filthy. They talk about the coming baby and the other children. Elizabeth tells John that Giles Corey has been executed by 'pressing' (laying heavy stones onto his chest). She says that he would not plead either guilty or not guilty to his charges and by this legal device he did not forfeit his property. Thus he died able to bequeath his property to his children.

They talk about him confessing, but she leaves the decision up to him. She forgives him but says he must forgive himself. He decides to confess, but baulks at the news that he must sign his name to the confession and it will be hung on the church door. He signs, but then crumples it up. He says: 'Because it is my name! Because I cannot have another in my life!' Then he says 'now I do think I see some goodness in John Proctor.' What is the goodness? He is being true to himself and his name, and he is refusing to sign his name to lies.

Danforth's last words are: 'Hang them high over the town! Who weeps for these, weeps for corruption!'

Parris and Hale both plead with Elizabeth to intercede but she says 'He have his goodness now. God forbid I take it from him.' The effect is that both Parris and Hale have fallen victim, in different ways, to the trials and the corruption. Elizabeth and John Proctor have risen above it, because of their love and because they maintain their integrity by refusing to sign to lies.

The drum is heard, heralding the executions.

SETTING

Setting is vital to the effect of *The Crucible.* As discussed in 'Context' above, the play is set in Salem Massachusetts, USA, in 1692. This setting is very specific, because what arises is only possible in a theocracy based on a very literal Christianity.

If you changed the setting of *The Crucible* it would not have the same meaning. One of the reasons for this is that the events that occurred in Salem in 1692 have entered into American history and folklore, making Salem a symbol of witchcraft and also of injustice based on superstition.

Miller, in *The Crucible,* is using the well-known story of the 'witches' of Salem in order to draw comparisons with events in his own time – the Communist 'witch hunts' of the early 1950s, driven by Senator Joseph McCarthy and his House Committee for Un-American Activities. As we know, Miller himself was called before the committee, so the issue was personal to him and some of his friends. He is clear when he shows that the collective experiences of the past are repeated in the present with the same ideas and mistakes being repeated.

Why didn't Miller simply write a play set in the 1950s about Communists and suspected Communists being persecuted for their opinions and the people with whom they associated? There are two good reasons for this.

The first is that the issue was highly divisive at the time and it became dangerous to even argue tolerance of Communists in public. A play like that would have put Miller at great risk.

The second reason is really much more important. By 1953 (when the play was first published), the Salem witch trials were accepted as based on foolish superstition that caused great injustice. It was accepted everywhere that most, probably all, of the people executed were entirely innocent. Therefore, if Miller could get his audience to see the similarities between the Salem trials and the McCarthy's arguments and techniques, then hopefully they would see that McCarthy's techniques were also unjust and based on superstition and fear. For example, if you are sitting in the theatre watching *The Crucible*, and you are wondering how on earth anyone can take Abigail's performance about 'the bird' (Act 3) seriously, then you might also wonder at a similar 'performance' by a witness in one of McCarthy's investigations. Another good example is the tendency for people to confess to anything in *The Crucible* in order to avoid hanging, or to name others if that helps. Similarly, one way out of a Communist investigation was to give the committee more names to investigate. Significantly, Miller himself refused to do this when he was interviewed.

THEMATIC CONCERNS

The Collective Experience

When we, as the audience, first enter the world of Salem Massachusetts, 1692, it appears to be a close-knit community based on being in a group or closed society. Belonging to this society, as in many societies, seems to depend on conformity to rules and shared beliefs, experiences and attitudes. We know that Christianity holds these people in check, and we quickly come to understand that it is a fairly strict Christianity, based on a literal reading of *The Bible*. We soon learn, for example, that dancing is not allowed. This literal reading of the Bible includes a belief in the existence, in a very real way, of the devil.

As well as this, we come to understand that the Church and the legal system work hand in hand, in what is called a 'theocracy'. Though this word is not used in the play, the concept is evident. In this sense, similarity of experience, especially public appearance, is *enforced* in Salem. Or, there is an attempt to enforce it, at least. Everyone is meant to have the same beliefs and everyone conforms to the same social values.

At the very beginning of the play, though, the audience comes upon the Reverend Parris in an odd posture of frantic prayer and we soon realise that all is not as it might seem. The very representative of God and God's word in the township is battling off accusations that his own daughter Betty is suffering the effects of contact with the devil. Parris, who is concerned about his status and security in the community as it is, does not want his name further tainted by the presence of the devil in his very own house.

Not long after, we learn that a group of girls have been found dancing in the woods—someone was even seen naked! On the one occasion that Abigail and the girls speak to each other in private, the audience hears that Parris' servant Tituba was in fact making a spell to make contact with Thomas and Anne Putnam's dead children. There is also talk of Abigail having drunk a charm to kill 'Goody Proctor'.

Next we meet John Proctor and find that he is a married man who has had an affair with 17-year-old Abigail Williams, who is still in love with him, hence the drinking of the charm. Proctor and Giles obviously don't like the Reverend Parris, and they joke about joining a faction to remove him, if such a faction really does exist.

Barely half-way through the first Act, the audience can see that, although Salem is *supposed to be* a place of general collective experience, it is quite something else under the surface. Reverend Hale of Beverley arrives, an expert at detecting and eradicating the devil. By the end of Act 1, Abigail and the other girls are in what appears to be some kind of trance, accusing an ever-increasing group of citizens of being devil-worshippers.

Does anyone in *The Crucible* actually 'belong' in Salem society? The answer to this will depend on the various experiences that we read about as we move through the text. The public and private experiences become indistinguishable as secrets and lies are brought to light. The individual experience is turned against that person and near anarchy is loosed in Salem.

The Human Experiences of Marriage

There are four marriages that are held up to scrutiny in *The Crucible* — the Proctors, the Nurses, the Putnams and the Coreys. Each of these marriages is put under pressure in some way or other and all of them actually stay together, though three are separated by death. We will look at how each of these experiences contributes to our understanding and what Miller is exposing / explaining about society through these marriages.

The Proctors

When we first see the Proctors, there is a good deal of distance between them, as a result of John's having had an affair with Abigail Williams who had formerly been their domestic help. John accuses Elizabeth of being unforgiving: 'You forget nothin' and forgive nothin' (p 55) but she responds that 'The magistrate sits in your heart that judges you. I never thought you but a good man John – [with a smile] – only somewhat bewildered.'

At this point in the play, the audience isn't sure who is right and who is wrong, but it is fair to say that Elizabeth's words and behaviour are consistent to what she says throughout the play. It *is* John who judges himself as immoral and she *does* regard him as a good man who made a mistake, not a bad man whose badness is reflected in his adultery. It is an emotional and confusing experience for both of them and it's not something they have experienced before.

Initially, it is Proctor's intention to stay out of what is happening in town – the accusations of witchcraft and the court procedures. Elizabeth suspects that this is because Abigail is involved and she is probably right. But he is also probably right in thinking that the safest thing to do is stay out of it and hope it blows over.

Proctor's hand is forced when Elizabeth, as she predicts, is arrested and accused. The bonds of marriage mean that he must go to the court to discredit Abigail and save Elizabeth.

His commitment to saving Elizabeth is such that he actually confesses to lechery with Abigail in a last ditch attempt to discredit her. 'It is a whore!' and 'I have known her, sir' (p 97) Elizabeth's commitment to John is such that when she is called in she lies for him (something she never does) and denies that he is a lecher. Thus the married couple have damned themselves, each in the attempt to save the other. The marriage bond is very powerful here and it transcends other values, such as the truth and public honour.

This extremely dramatic moment in Act 3 galvanises Elizabeth and John as a couple committed to each other, even though the upshot of it is that they are separated and both sentenced to death.

When next they are together, in Act 4, Elizabeth has been sent in to convince Proctor to sign a confession that (really) everybody knows is false. If she has not forgiven him before, she certainly does now, taking the blame for his adultery herself: 'It needs a cold wife to prompt lechery.' (p 119)

Aside from sending feminists into a rage, this line, by anyone's standards, is a generous one. It is an attempt to put the experience to rest, at last. Both have learnt something from the experience but it costs John his life.

In the end, Elizabeth has the love, strength and wisdom to let John make his own decision. His repulsion at having his name shamed by having his confession hung on the church overrides his desire to live and see his children grow.

I think we can say that marriage does function as an agent of experience for Elizabeth and John Proctor, even when he chooses death. He makes this choice with her blessing and permission to do so. It isn't the decision she wants, but she wants more for him to do what is in his heart. 'He have his goodness now. God forbid I take it from him.' (p 126)

The Nurses

Rebecca Nurse is the representation of goodness in the play. She belongs with God, no matter what anyone else says. She also belongs in her marriage with Francis.

Francis goes to the court thinking to save his wife but comes up against a brick wall in the person of Deputy Governor Danforth whose self-importance makes him a very bad judge of character. (For example, he believes Abigail and does not believe Rebecca.) Francis has a statement of support for Rebecca signed by ninety-one 'covenanted Christians' to present to Danforth. To his dismay, Danforth calls for the ninety-one to be summoned to the court and investigated.

Nothing can shake Rebecca's faith in God or her love for Francis. For her to live by signing an untrue confession is completely unthinkable to her, so she goes untroubled to her death. Her experience shows us that it is the innocent that are hurt by the collective experiences in the town.

The Coreys

To his eternal regret, Giles Corey asks Reverend Hale an innocent question about his wife reading so much and the next thing he knows she is under suspicion. Who would have thought that reading would be identified as witchcraft? This shows us that the experience of witch-hunting in Salem has gone too far and that all logic has been dismissed in the quest for 'God'.

Giles own behaviour at the court soon has him identified as an opponent of it and therefore a suspect. His refusal to declare whether he is innocent or guilty prevents his forfeiting his land, so that he protects his family from ruin by allowing himself to be pressed to death with heavy stones.

The Putnams

Respected members of the community, they do belong in Salem society initially. It soon becomes apparent that they are profiting from the actions of the court, as convicted witches forfeit their land and the Putnams can seize it. They stick together as well, so they share the experiences as a married couple.

It seems clear that Ann Putnam has Tituba conjure spirits in an attempt to find a reason for the fact that seven of her babies have died in infancy. She is prepared to believe that it is the devil at work, through his agents in Salem. The experience of the loss of her infants has made her suspicious and bitter – she has personal and emotive reasons for acting in the way she does without making it right.

The Collective Experience - Peers

The peer group is often an agent of collective experiences, as it is in *The Crucible*. Young unmarried females apparently have no status at all in Salem society, so it is not surprising that they have formed some kind of peer group. What is surprising is that they have met at night in the woods and engaged in dancing, running naked and some kind of conjuring of spirits. Abigail's addresses to the others (pages 25-27) tell the audience that, as well, she has drunk a charm to kill Goody (Elizabeth) Proctor.

Abigail threatens the others and instructs them to admit to having danced, but nothing else.

This peer group exists because they are all ostracised from Salem society. They can be house girls, but little else, until they marry. (One of the peculiarities about the play is that there don't appear to be any young males in Salem – well, they don't crop up in the play, anyway.)

It is this peer group that gets behind Abigail and supports her (mainly, it would seem, out of fear) in the 'crying out' at the end of Act 1 when they name the names of women in the town who are witches. So Abigail, Mercy Lewis, Mary Warren, Betty Parris, Ruth Putnam and the others all experience things in this peer group in a way that they cannot anywhere else in Salem society. This has to do with self-expression. In Salem they are expected to keep their heads down and say little. Even our hero, John Proctor is intolerant of them showing any initiative, threatening to discipline Mary Warren if she does not do what she is told.

From the time of the first accusations, right through to the end of Act 3, this peer group, led by Abigail, becomes effectively the centre of Salem society. What they say goes. As Danforth recognises, once he has hanged one person on their evidence, he is obliged to hang everybody else that they accuse, even if one of them is Rebecca Nurse, whom no one at all can believe could be guilty. Even Danforth himself dares not challenge Abigail.

The power of this peer group as an agent of collective experience is best demonstrated in Act 3 when Mary Warren, at Proctor's insistence, goes to the court to tell Danforth that it is all pretence and that she has not, in fact, seen any witches, spirits or devils. Mary is trying to belong with the Proctors and with adult Salem society in general – a kind of experience which she is normally excluded from.

Danforth puts a lot of pressure on her to be sure that her story is true, and in effect tries to bully her into changing her story, that it is all pretence, but she holds firm with Proctor's support.

But, when Abigail 'sees' the bird, then talks to it as though it is Mary, she is able to turn the pressure of the peer group onto Mary. The girls break her down by repeating in unison everything she says, and eventually Mary turns on Proctor, calling him 'the devil's man'.

So, the power of the peer group as an agent of influence is demonstrated. Mary would rather lie about Proctor and see the others hanged than be excluded from the peer group. One of the reasons for this is that the peer group has been the only agent of different experiences that Mary has had access to. She is too young to be a member of the Salem community in some other way. She has no other way of experiencing more of life and being part of a group.

By Act 4, everything has dispersed and the group no longer exists. Abigail and Mercy have stolen money from Parris and run away. Danforth realises how ridiculous this makes the court look, but presses on with the hangings anyway.

You could argue, that Abigail and the young-female peer group are exactly what Salem society deserves, because their position is a by-product of the strictness and hypocrisy of Salem. They wield so much power because of the superstitious beliefs that hold the theocracy together. Hale comes looking for the devil, and Abigail just gives him what he wants. There is no status in Salem between 'child' and 'wife', so Abigail grasps control of things in the only way she can. It also saves her being whipped for dancing.

What we can see from all this is that being part of a collective or group experience is a human instinct or need and part of the idea of what makes humanity. The girls belong as a peer group and the group is able to have a powerful control over its members, such as Mary Warren, and everyone else, for a time. Belonging to the peer group is the only way they can engage in experiences otherwise forbidden to them. These experiences, at least for a short time, give their lives meaning. Here we see both positive and negative qualities that define the society and the varied motivations that change their and our assumptions about the world.

The Religious Experience

Religion is the thing that everyone in Salem society agrees about, so it ought to be a positive experience. It should bring people together. But it actually doesn't, for the most part. Why?

One of the biggest problems is Reverend Parris. Instead of bringing the community together through Christian faith and beliefs, he is a cause of conflict because the kind of man that he is.

For one thing, his life does not exhibit Christian values. He is selfish and insecure in his position. He covets things like golden candlesticks, which has alienated some members of the congregation. Proctor says that when he preaches it is all 'hell fire and damnation' and he never mentions God. Proctor says that this is why people (like him) don't want to attend church. Parris shows no concern for the condition of his daughter Betty at the beginning of the play; all he cares about is that her condition and the rumours could be bad for his reputation in the community.

Parris' lowest point is probably when he lies in court, denying that he saw anyone naked in the woods, when the audience knows he did. His 'concern' that Proctor confess and live is entirely based on the fear that Proctor's death might cause people to blame Parris in some way and make his position even less tenable.

Even Danforth finds him intolerable. Parris is not the kind of man who is going to unite the community or spread a true Christian message as his personal experience belies his faith.

The other thing is that, of the characters that we meet in the play, very few of them seem genuinely motivated by Christian values. Rebecca and Francis Nurse and Elizabeth Proctor seem the only ones. The Putnams are motivated by bitterness and greed. Giles believes that they instructed their daughter Ruth to 'cry out' against people whose land they can then take.

Though the inhabitants of Salem would tell you that their whole society is based on Christian beliefs, basic Christian values have been distorted in Salem. Real goodness in a person is set against trivial indicators like the keeping of poppets or the memorising of the Ten Commandments. This is because the court is dealing in 'invisibles' and superstition, not evidence and facts. This problem is inherent in any situation where a court tries to adjudicate on beliefs or something else that cannot be seen or heard. Faith is a personal experience that has been made a public spectacle and the issue with this is tangible in the play. Public displays of Christian ethos may bely what the individual is thinking.

OTHER ASPECTS OF HUMAN EXPERIENCE

The Experience of Inclusion and Exclusion

One of the most important elements that lead to the injustices and destructiveness of the situation in Salem is that young people are **excluded** from the society. This pushes them together, encourages rebellion (dancing and so on in the woods) and causes them to enjoy the way they are treated in the court. They give Hale and Danforth the accused and they are given respect. We see this very clearly in Mary Warren, who tells Proctor that she will not tolerate being punished by him any more.

In fact, **exclusion** is a much more common factor in Salem than **inclusion**. Any one unusual or non-conformist is excluded from the collective experience. As well, being accused of being a witch is a very real way of being excluded and this is happening to an ever-increasing group of people as the play proceeds. Rebecca Nurse is an inclusive person, she likes everyone and treats everyone well.

Choosing to Ignore the Collective Experience

In *The Crucible*, many characters are pushed into a position of not being part of the community as it tries to ensure religious purity, but there are some instances of characters making a choice not to participate in that experience.

When we meet John Proctor he is an individualist, choosing not to belong to the church congregation, blaming his dislike of the preaching of Reverend Parris.

Giles has followed a road in life based on individualism also, and you could say that he chooses not to belong in Salem society.

As matters develop, Proctor is forced to go to the court to save Elizabeth. When things don't go as he expected, he is forced to play his 'trump card', attempting to discredit Abigail as a witness by labelling her a whore on the grounds that he has 'slept' with her. You would have to say that, in doing this, he is deliberately forfeiting his social status as a member of that society for a higher purpose – love and marriage.

Likewise, Elizabeth, in lying to Danforth about John's lechery, thinking that she is saving John's reputation, is deliberately putting in great jeopardy her own social belonging.

Reverend Hale chooses not to continue as part of the theocratic experience at the end of Act 3 when he denounces the court and walks out. He makes this choice on the basis of his own conscience and that he feels responsible to some extent for what is happening. He sees that Danforth is giving the accused no chance of defending themselves and that Abigail is of dubious character.

Danforth's attempt to get Proctor to confess at the end is a kind of offer of a redemptive experience – Proctor can return to Salem life with his wife and children and belong again. Proctor rejects this and in doing so he is choosing not to belong. Proctor sees the price of being part of society as being the public ruin of his name, a price he baulks at paying.

Attitudes to Human Experiences

The principal examples of this are Reverend Hale and Abigail Williams.

As discussed above, Hale arrives in Salem, as a community leader. He is full of confidence and pride. By the end of Act 3 his attitude to the whole process has changed because he sees the court as not operating for justice. He deliberately walks out of the court, rejecting his position in it. The experience has altered his ideas and assumptions about the theocratic process and he vehemently rejects the manner in which the court has taken truth away and made power the primary factor.

The case of Abigail is quite different. Her original plan is to become part of the community by replacing Elizabeth Proctor as John Proctor's lover. Thus she would be a wife and belong in Salem as an adult. But John thwarts this plan too because he loves his wife, despite his adultery. His own life experiences and integrity make him see his initial folly and reject Abigail – he sees her for the manipulative person she is.

Abigail tries drinking a charm to kill Elizabeth, but with Reverend Hale and Danforth arriving in town, she has to cover the traces of that action, so she seeks inculcate herself with the theocrats by becoming the lead actress in a sham where innocent people are sent to their deaths on her word and the word of the other girls whom she leads. She achieves recognition and status in the court because of the false experiences she creates. The final act of this phase of status is to participate in the damning of the man she once loved – John Proctor.

When Act 4 opens, Parris has the news that Abigail and Mercy Lewis have stolen money from him and left town.

So, the modifications over time of Abigail's attitude to the world are that she goes from coveting recognition and position desperately, to achieving it in the court and wielding with gusto the power that it brings, and finally to escaping the experience she had falsely created. Presumably she and Mercy set off to find some other kind of life experience somewhere else.

Here Miller is showing us that these experiences she creates because of self-interest are harmful to the society that she wants to join. Her egotistical manipulations are all about Abigail and are not for the benefit of the society. Eventually these experiences are seen as false and her position is in jeopardy so she runs away, taking the last remnants of her poisoning with her. Unfortunately it is too late for some but hopefully the community will be the wiser for the experiences, as will some of the individuals such as Hale.

Human Experiences and Identity in The Crucible

John Proctor is the central character of *The Crucible* and its hero. In the play and in the real world there is a sense in which we are all seeking a peace and acceptance of ourselves through experiences, both positive and negative. The experiences change our assumptions and ideas about people and the world. It is actually this aspect of the play that is most pertinent to a study of John Proctor.

When we first see John Proctor in town, he is a man who holds himself well and looks like he does not gladly tolerate fools. But in the short conversation that he has with Abigail, the audience learns that he has sinned with her, and he is not comfortable about it. His claim to Abigail that 'we never touched' is a plea for mercy and forgetfulness that shows his vulnerability. Abigail still wants him, and though he turns her away it is with difficulty and not absolute conviction.

In Act 2 we see that his wife Elizabeth has a keen understanding that it is guilt and shame that stand in the way of him coming to terms with himself. Elizabeth offers forgiveness, but Proctor doesn't quite believe her and he isn't prepared to believe that she should forgive him.

In Act 3 they each sacrifice their social reputation in an attempt to protect the other. He admits to lechery with Abigail and Elizabeth tells a lie, thinking that he will avoid having to admit to lechery (which he has already done.) Thus they each demonstrate absolute commitment to the other.

In Act 4, Elizabeth claims responsibility for John's unfaithfulness. Initially he decides that he is not worthy to die with the likes of Rebecca Nurse, but he baulks at the fact that his confession will be hung publicly on the church door. This arousal of his pride and concern for his name causes him to retract the confession and go to the gallows. Importantly, he says: 'You have made your magic now, for now I do see some shred of goodness in John Proctor. Not enough to weave a banner with but white enough to keep it from such dogs' (p 125).

They kiss with passion and Elizabeth understands that 'he have his goodness now.' For Proctor, this acceptance of himself and renewed sense of his own identity is the key to show how the experiences he has undergone in the course of the play have made him understand himself in new ways.

Questions on Human Experiences

1. Define the term human experiences in your own words and apply this definition to *The Crucible*.
2. Name ONE specific character and show how TWO specific experiences shape their destiny and the destiny of those around them. Use specific quotes from the text to support your ideas.
3. Discuss how the collective experiences in the play shape the ideas that Miller is conveying? You can think about both the negative and the positive experiences that the community has.
4. How do you see the concept of marriage in the text in terms of experience? Choose ONE particular relationship to use in support of your ideas.
5. Analyse the role of 'religious experience' in *The Crucible* in terms of the human experience. Think about the way in which religion is a dominant idea and practice in Salem.
6. Explain the role of the inclusion and exclusion in the play? Why might some people choose exclusion from an experience?
7. While we are focused on human experiences as our main idea we also need to think about other concepts that integrate into this idea. Choose ONE and develop a thesis for it with specific reference to *The Crucible*.
8. What did you learn from reading the play about human experiences that might be applicable to your world?

OTHER THEMES LINKED TO HUMAN EXPERIENCES IN *THE CRUCIBLE*

Generational Rebellion

What happens in *The Crucible* can be seen as the young people rebelling against the rules of the older people. Clearly young people have no freedom and no power in Salem society. Proctor threatens to beat Mary Warren if she does not do his bidding. Abigail has aspirations to be John Proctor's wife and to be taken seriously as an adult. It is Abigail who recognises the potential power of the young girls in the circumstances and musters them to wield that power. In Act 3 it becomes apparent that Abigail can threaten anyone, including Deputy Governor Danforth. If she were to accuse him of witchcraft, how could he deny the truth of it, seeing he has sent others to jail, and hanged some, on the girls' accusations?

It is Proctor who best recognises the situation, saying: 'and now the little crazy children are jangling the keys to the kingdom, and common vengeance writes the law.' He identifies the courtroom system as a 'role reversal' where the young people have usurped their elders and taken over running things.

In a less repressive society (note, for example, the hysterical attitude to dancing) the 'children' are less likely to turn on the adults.

Vengeance

Vengeance is usually the result of some kind of specific conflict, but it is never the resolution of it.

Ann Putnam is looking for someone to blame for the death of her babies, and she harbours deep jealousy for those who have many healthy children. Thomas Putnam looks to settle old scores to his own advantage by grabbing the land of those accused.

Most importantly, Abigail seeks vengeance on Elizabeth Proctor for sacking her from her job at the Proctors' and thus removing her from the object of her desires – John Proctor. It seems clear enough that she drank a potion made by Tituba in order to put a curse on Elizabeth. When the naming of the devil's agents begins, Elizabeth knows that Abigail will call her out, and she is right.

Interpersonal Relationships

There is conflict between Parris and Proctor, Corey and Putnam. None of the three men has any respect for him. There is also conflict between he and his niece Abigail as she tries to keep from him the truth about what happened in the woods. The Putnams seem to be at war with everybody. They claim the land of others, and Ann is bitter at the loss of her seven children.

There is conflict between Proctor and Abigail as she wants their relationship to continue and he has decided that it must not. There is conflict between Abigail and Elizabeth Proctor over John. Elizabeth quickly realises that Abigail wants to remove her so she can have John. Abigail drinks a charm of Tituba's to kill Elizabeth, then calls her out as a witch.

Judge Hathorn and Deputy Governor Danforth act to preserve the apparent rectitude of the court, and this brings them into conflict with Proctor, Giles Corey and Francis Nurse. Danforth is put into a position where he must avoid conflict with Abigail, or all the convictions might fall down.

The most important interpersonal conflict in the play is between Elizabeth and John Proctor. When we first see them together in Act 2 there is a distance and awkwardness between them which stems from John having committed adultery with Abigail, seven months before. Elizabeth has not really forgiven him, and he is even further from forgiving himself. Her arrest at the end of Act 2 brings them together in a sense, as he realises how much she means to him and also he demonstrates that he will do anything to bring her back. As we see, this includes the destruction of his own good name in public. In Act 3, Elizabeth lies to Danforth (something that Proctor has said she is incapable of doing) rather than say that John is a lecher. In Act 4, Danforth allows them some time together in the hopes that she will convince him to 'confess'. It is in this scene that they make peace with each other and she refuses to influence his decision about confessing. In the end, he does not confess, choosing to hang. Elizabeth, very wisely, says to Hale 'He have his goodness now. God forbid I take it from him.'

Conscience and Internal Conflict

In Act 1, Reverend John Hale is the picture of self-assurance and confidence. There is no internal conflict at this stage. By the end of Act 2 he is starting to have doubts, feeling that obviously good people are being arrested. During Act 3 he starts to see that there is no way that the accused can defend themselves without either accusing someone else or being accused of trying to bring the court down. At the end of Act 3, he denounces the proceedings and quits the court. In Act 4 he is a broken man, going around trying, as he puts it, to counsel Christians to tell lies (by confessing to witchcraft that they haven't done). At the end he is riddled with guilt and doubt as he begs Elizabeth to convince John to 'confess' and avoid the noose. He feels responsible for the death of innocent people.

In Act 1, John Proctor is clearly still intrigued by Abigail, but just as determined not to give in to her desires for him. In Act 2 we see the source of his internal conflict as Elizabeth has not forgiven him and he hasn't forgiven himself for having had a sexual relationship with Abigail while she was working for them. He doesn't want to get involved with the court, but his hand is forced when Elizabeth is arrested. He goes to the court intending to denounce Abigail by saying that she said that it was all 'sport', not witchcraft. When this fails, in a desperate attempt to unseat Abigail and save Elizabeth, he admits to having 'known her'. Proctor's internal conflict plays out to the very end of the play, where he finally refuses to allow the confession to be hung on the church door, and tears it up. He goes to his death believing that he has done the right thing: 'now I do think I see some shred of goodness in John Proctor.' Elizabeth's selfless wisdom has allowed him to make the decision that finally rids him of his internal conflict.

The social peer pressure that falls on Mary Warren makes her situation one of internal conflict. You can 'read' her as responding to external forces, but she is still experiencing internal conflict. She is frightened of Proctor and goes to the court because of him, but still I think she knows that she is doing the right thing.

Danforth threatens her on two or three occasions, but she holds the line. But, Abigail and the other girls apply such pressure on her that in the end she buckles, and, for self-preservation, turns it all back on Proctor, calling him the devil's man.

Something must be said under internal conflict about Elizabeth Proctor. When we meet her, there is a lot going on in her life, but I would say that she has clear ideas and attitudes. She distrusts Abigail, doesn't really trust John yet and doesn't really believe in witches. When she is called into the vestry to testify, she tries very hard to answer Danforth's questions without either putting John in jeopardy or lying. When this becomes impossible, she chooses to lie rather than reveal her husband's lechery. In the scene where Danforth cross-examines her, you can say that she is encountering internal conflict, or you could say that she in fact knows clearly what she wants to do, but that Danforth won't let her get away with it. In Act 4 she admits to John that 'it needs a cold wife to prompt lechery.' This indicates to us that she has reassessed her role in John's relationship with Abigail and could indicate internal conflict. Just the same, the way from there on is clear to her and she steadfastly refuses to influence John's decision to confess or not, and even Hale's pleadings at the very end do not turn her from that path. You need to decide for yourself whether you would count her as experiencing internal conflict.

It is interesting to note that (I think) none of the other characters does seem to experience internal conflict. They all seem to me to hold the line of what they believe in (Rebecca, Giles) or what they want to achieve (Abigail, Danforth).

While the whole situation in *The Crucible* is set up by social conflict caused by the repressive Salem culture, in my opinion, **internal**

conflict is the most powerful of the many types of conflict in the play. Because we understand the varied pressures on Proctor's conscience, his moment of admission of lechery with Abigail and Elizabeth's subsequent denial, are very powerful dramatically. Likewise, the change in Hale, though gradual, is so great that it has a huge impact on the play. When Hale denounces the court, no one in the audience would disagree with him. Mary Warren's timid desperation to hold the line and be with God, buckles under the pressure of Danforth's bullying and Abigail's frightening influence on her and the other girls. This scene is a crucial one, and it demonstrates the power of peer social pressure.

For a while in Act 2, Proctor's conscience is telling him to go to the court and his good sense is telling him to keep well out of it. This changes when Elizabeth is arrested and he is forced to go to the court to try to save her.

The most interesting observation about consciences in the play, is that so many characters don't seem to have one at all – Abigail, Danforth, the Putnams, Parris and Mercy Lewis, at least. The irony is that for its entire apparent adherence to 'Christian Law', Salem society is nearly a 'conscience-free zone'!

Freedom and Repression

These two concepts are set against each other in the play. Salem in 1692 is a society based on repression and the lack of individual freedom. This situation is about to 'break out' (as repression will do) at the start of the play. By the end of Act 1, the girls are giving full vent to their repressed energies. This continues in Act 3 where Danforth cannot control it and Mary Warren cannot stand up against it. By Act 4, Abigail has truly exercised her new-found freedom by leaving Salem altogether.

Truth and Lies

Again there is a natural juxtaposition here. Initially, Abigail tells part of the truth to Parris, but far from all. We learn what seems to be the truth during her conversations with Mercy Lewis and Mary Warren – that there was dancing and the conjuring by Tituba of the spirits of Ruth Putnam's dead siblings. Also, that Abigail drank a charm to kill Goody Proctor and that Mercy Lewis was naked. Abigail confesses to the lesser of the crimes, dancing, and puts Tituba in for conjuring. Then she shrewdly concocts a situation where the girls are the innocent victims of the devil and his agents Sarah Good, Goody Osburn and the others.

The other interesting aspect of truth is that the only way an accused can avoid hanging is to confess. Naturally, in such circumstances, you'd have to wonder about the truth of the confessions. By the end of the play, it is clear that no-one believes in the truth of the confessions, but Danforth allows Elizabeth and John to be together in the hopes that Proctor will sign one. This is highly hypocritical of Danforth, who should not accept what he knows is a false confession.

The Law, the Courts and Justice

These institutions are supposed to operate together for good, but the situation in Salem very quickly becomes one where one injustice leads to another. If the accusations of the girls are believed once, then they must be believed every time. Once a person is accused, the only way to save themselves is to confess. Each confession is a validation of the accusations of the girls.

It is clear that Judge Danforth understands the problems of dispensing justice in these circumstances. Only he can do something about it, but he knows that if he does it will cast doubt on the convictions that have already been made.

In Act 3, Danforth makes an important speech about the legal implications of the Salem situation. 'I should be confounded were I called upon to defend these people.' He goes on to explain that because witchcraft is an invisible crime, only the witch and the victim can know about it. We can't rely on the witch to testify, so we have to rely on the victim, 'and they do testify.' In other words, once the court accepts that the girls are victims, then anyone they accuse must be a witch. When the accused claim that they are not witches, well, that's just what we'd expect them to do. Anyone who supports them must be suspect too.

Social Authority vs Individual Conscience

This is often said to be the central theme of the play.

In Salem 1692, social authority is so rigid and all encompassing that there is really no room at all for an individual to exercise their own conscience or value system. People like Proctor, Rebecca and Giles come into conflict with the court as a representative of society because they want the right to exercise their own conscience. This is why we sympathise with them against Parris, the Putnams and Danforth. The play warns us of what can happen to an individual's 'right' to express his or her own opinion in a social circumstance where dogma is rigid and unable to be questioned. It is a warning that we should never lose sight of.

refers back to Twilight again in a use of dry humour when a boy shows interest in her:

Think about some of the key Human Experiences in *The Crucible* and analyse how these Human Experiences are represented in the text.

Number	Select a key human experience from *The Crucible*	What language techniques are used to represent the human experience? Find quotes to support.
1		
2		
3		

Number	Select a key human experience from *The Crucible*	What language techniques are used to represent the human experience? Find quotes to support.
4		
5		

What are some of the key ideas flowing from the human experiences and their representation in the text?

Some of the key ideas flowing from the human experiences represented in *The Crucible* might be:

- Freedom and repression
- Leadership – particularly by religious and leading citizens
- Courage and Speaking Out in the face of fear
- Religion and Religious Extremism
- Truth and Lies

What other key ideas flow from the representation of human experiences in the text?

Select three ideas flowing from the human experiences in the text (use some from above or your own) to unpack in a paragraph below. Find quotes from the text relevant to each key idea.

Key Idea	Quotes

Further Reading:

t

CHARACTER ANALYSIS

Each of the characters shows us something about human experiences individually but it is with their interactions that we see the reality of how these experiences impact upon dealings with others and on the community. Miller explores with each of these characters some aspect of the human condition – with flaws and without — that shows us something about ourselves. These assessments are only brief as much has been covered in the previous section.

John Proctor

John Proctor is a Salem farmer. He is a proud man with his own opinions, making him a man who will attract trouble in a society that expects everyone to be the same.

He is also a fallen man in his own estimation, having committed adultery with 17 year-old Abigail when she was his wife's assistant in their house. As we see early in the play, his relationship with Abigail is over as far as he is concerned, but not as far as she is concerned.

When his wife Elizabeth is arrested, he knows that he must go to the court and invalidate Abigail's testimony. Initially, it is merely his intention to say that Abigail told him that what happened in the woods was mere 'sport', not witchcraft. In doing this he is attacking her credibility and surrendering his own respectability. It is characteristic of Salem as a theocracy that the revelation that Abigail is not a virgin would reflect immediately on the validity of her testimony.

As Proctor gets caught up in the injustice of the court, in order to discredit her, he eventually admits to having had relations with Abigail. She and the girls turn on him and he is accused of being 'the devil's man'.

In Act 4, the action centres on whether he will 'confess' and thus be saved from hanging. He and Elizabeth make their peace, but in the end he refuses to have the confession hung on the church door, crumples it up and goes to his death believing that he has shown some goodness in doing this.

Proctor's is the story of a man with great pride who has fallen below his own standards. Ultimately, he rises above those around him and goes to his death rather than falsely damn his own name by confessing to what he hasn't done.

Miller has written Proctor as the hero of the play. He is a flawed hero, but his decision at the end to stand up for the truth and his own name is seen by Miller as one of courage. He is a very American hero – like the hero in a cowboy movie of the 1950s.

Elizabeth Proctor

It is said that Elizabeth is the personification of faith in marriage. She lies in the court before Danforth in order to try to save her husband from the embarrassment of having his lechery generally known. At the end she refuses to beg him to confess and live, allowing him to make his own decision, and die.

At the end she has the wisdom to understand that John has found peace within himself and that it would be wrong of her to take it away. 'He have his goodness now. God forbid I take it from him.' (p 126)

Abigail

Abigail is the 17-year-old niece of Reverend Parris. Seven months before the play begins she has been removed from her job at the Proctors by Elizabeth, because of the sexual relationship she has had with John.

In a scene in Act 1, she makes it clear to John Proctor that she wants for them to be together again. She also tells him that there was no witchcraft involved in the goings-on in the woods. The audience already knows from the previous scene that this isn't true, that she had drunk a charm to kill Elizabeth Proctor.

In order to deflect the accusations about what she did on that night, she accuses Tituba of conjuring spirits. When this works, she takes the next step and leads the girls in accusing Sarah Good and Goody Osburn of working with the devil and sending their spirits out on her. Once the court has convicted someone on the evidence of the girls, then it must continue to convict, and it does.

Thus, Abigail becomes the most powerful figure in the play, even able to intimidate Danforth.

It is difficult to closely assess her motives and especially her development as the early scene between her and Proctor is the only one where she might be behaving naturally, reflective of her true self. (And even in that scene, she doesn't tell Proctor the whole truth.) There can be little doubt that she is a consummate actress. She also appears to have the ability to intimidate and rule the other girls. 'I have seen some reddish work done at night' (p 27) is a threat of violence if they don't do as she says.

In the end, she doesn't get Proctor, but she does avoid a whipping for dancing, and she gets out of Salem with Parris' money. Her testimony sends many innocent people to their deaths, but many audience members would be more inclined to blame Danforth for that.

Reverend Hale

In some ways, Hale is the most interesting character in the play, because he changes (develops) so much. He enters Salem like some hero/saviour, entirely confident in his knowledge and ability to find and defeat Satan. From this position of confidence, he falls. He is shaken by the arrests of Elizabeth and Rebecca, as he believed them to be innocent.

He gradually comes to the realisation that there is no way for the accused to defend themselves in the court. He quits the court at the end of Act 3, disillusioned and frustrated. By the beginning of Act 4 he is a broken man, trying to convince prisoners to sign 'confessions', which he knows are false. He is hysterical with guilt as Proctor goes to the gallows.

Deputy Governor Danforth

It is consistent with Danforth's and society's beliefs that the Lord is speaking through the girls to identify devil-worshippers in Salem. Once he has convicted people on the 'evidence' of the girls, he must continue to go on doing so as he is incapable of admitting a mistake.

Danforth is proud and arrogant, full of his own self-importance. He explains to Hale why it is so difficult for the accused to defend themselves, but does nothing about it. He knows the confession of Proctor would be false, but pushes for it because it would be better politically. His arrogance shows in his dismissal of the idea of a postponement, as it would 'speaks a floundering.' His own image of his own power and judgement means everything. He does what he does in order to validate the court and the system. Hanging innocent people means less to him than preserving the system.

Mary Warren

Mary Warren is probably the most difficult character in the play to understand and the most difficult to play.

She is a little younger than Abigail and Mercy Lewis, and seems to wield no influence in the peer group. She is treated like a child by John Proctor and this is one reason why being the centre of attention and taken seriously in court appeals to her so much.

As far as we can tell, Proctor mainly bullies her into testifying against Abigail, though she does seem to have in her mind the idea that it is the right thing to do and that God is with her. She stands up pretty well to Danforth's attempts to bully and intimidate her, but she buckles in the end at the pressure exerted by Abigail and the other girls. It might come as a surprise, though, that she buckles to the point that she declares Proctor to be 'the devil's man.'

So Mary Warren goes from being Proctor's saviour to being his accuser. After that, we never hear of her again.

Giles Corey

Eighty years old, shrewd, argumentative and determined, Giles Corey is probably the most likeable character in the play. He has been in court 33 times and he knows the law and its procedures.

His innocent question about his wife reading books, leads to her (Martha) being accused of witchcraft, and this he cannot forgive himself for. He is pressed to death (heavy stones are placed onto his chest) for refusing to plead guilty or not guilty to witchcraft. By doing so he does not lose his property. So the old warrior has a victory of sorts in the end.

Rebecca Nurse

As Francis Nurse says: 'My wife is the very brick and mortar of the church.' (67) Rebecca is the symbol of goodness in the play. She is almost too good to be human. She goes to her death because she refuses to sign a false confession. As with Elizabeth, it comes as a shock to the audience when Rebecca is accused of witchcraft. The audience thinks that the charge is ridiculous and it works as a measure of how far away justice is from the goings on in the court. She offers support and some inspiration to Proctor at the end.

She says, as a warning to Danforth, 'Another judgment waits us all' (p 125) as she is being led to the gallows.

Reverend Samuel Parris

Parris cares only about his reputation and the insecurity of his position as the minister in Salem. There may not be an organised faction against him in the church, but it is clear that he is very unpopular. The two reasons that we hear about for this are that his sermons are all 'fire and brimstone' (all about the sufferings of hell) and that he preached for months about golden candlesticks until he had them.

On top of this, Parris is just plain annoying, he even annoys Danforth, who he supports. He is a snivelling coward who only cares about himself. He displays no loyalty to his congregation; rather he cheers the girls on as they damn many of them to be hanged. He lies in court when he says that he didn't see anyone naked in the woods.

At the end of the play, Parris is isolated and terrified that Proctor's hanging might back-fire on him.

DRAMATIC TECHNIQUES

As used by **Arthur Miller** in The Crucible

Dramatic Irony

In Act 1, the audience is privy to two scenes that allow us to get a reasonably clear idea of what really happened in the woods on the night in question and insight into Abigail's motives. The only character present at both of these is Abigail.

The first is the scene between Abigail, Mercy Lewis, Betty Parris and Mary Warren. From this scene we come to an understanding that the girls danced, Mercy Lewis was naked, Tituba tried to conjure the Putnam's dead children and Abigail drank a potion to kill Elizabeth Proctor.

The second is the scene between Abigail and Proctor, in which she attempts to arouse him sexually again, but also tells him that what happened in the woods was 'mere sport', fun. In this, she is not telling him the whole truth.

This sets up what is called 'Dramatic Irony'. Dramatic irony operates in a play when the audience knows more than the characters do. Only the girls and the audience know what happened in the woods, and only Proctor and Abigail know that she still expects them to be together. None of the adults in Salem, except Proctor and Elizabeth know that he had an affair with Abigail.

The main effect of this Dramatic Irony is that the audience is better able to assess Abigail's behaviour and motives than most of the other characters. It makes us more inclined to see the injustice of what is going on in court. We are more likely to see Abigail as manipulative and selfish, and a very good actress.

The audience is also better able to get the full dramatic impact of Proctor's confession to being a lecher and the sheer unexpected drama of Elizabeth's denial of it. This becomes one of the climaxes of the play.

The Manipulation of Tension

Miller plunges us directly into the tension, as the curtain opens to reveal Betty Parris inert on her bed with her father at her side praying. In Act 1, from this, there is a general rise in tension, culminating at the end with the hysteria of the girls crying out the names of those they accuse of witchcraft.

Act 2 opens with a calm and quiet scene between Elizabeth and John. Here the tension is not so dramatic, but is interpersonal tension between them. Again the pattern is a general rise in tension, culminating in Elizabeth's chaining and Proctor's promise to 'fall like an ocean on that court.'

Act 3 again begins in a more controlled fashion, by virtue of Danforth's presence, but the tension rises quickly as we realise that Mary Warren and Proctor attempting to discredit Abigail is more likely to bring about their own undoing. There is a huge climax when Elizabeth unexpectedly lies to 'protect' John. Then Mary Warren cracks under the pressure of the girls led by Abigail and accuses Proctor of being 'the devil's man'. Act 3 also ends with hysteria and a culmination of tension, Reverend Hale quitting the court.

Act 4 again begins slowly. Again there is a gradual rise of tension as both Danforth and Parris realise that if Rebecca Nurse and Proctor hang, there could be rebellion. Proctor's screwing up of his confession and Elizabeth's wise support makes the tension peak again at the end of Act 4.

Arthur Miller cleverly manipulates this tension in each Act, in order to get the maximum dramatic impact from the climaxes in his play.

Juxtaposition

Juxtaposition is a technique in all art that involves placing contrasting things side by side in order to heighten the awareness of the contrast.

For example, Rebecca Nurse's total goodness is juxtaposed with Parris' total badness. He makes her look better and she makes him look worse. Abigail is juxtaposed with Elizabeth. Abigail's 'love' for John is selfish lust, while Elizabeth's devotion is selfless, to the point where she is prepared to lie for him and prepared to allow him to find goodness and choose death at the end. Danforth and Corey are juxtaposed in terms of their attitudes to justice and the law.

The young people are juxtaposed to the older ones – they have a tribal unity that is extraordinarily powerful, while the adults can't agree on anything.

Light and Sound

In his published text, Miller is very specific about light and sound. The opening scene begins in candlelight, with a thin shaft of sunlight coming through a small window. The effect is one of mystery. Also, Parris, characteristically, is turned away from the light.

In Act 2, the darkness grows as the scene progresses. By the time Elizabeth is taken away it is dark. In Act 3 there is much more natural light, it is 'streaming' through two windows. By Act 4, the darkness has taken over, the figures in the scene are just heaps of rags. By the end the new sun is pouring in on Elizabeth's face, as her husband has 'found his goodness'. This is a positive image, even though Rebecca and John are about to die.

There are three sound devices worth mentioning. The first is the effect of the singing of the hymn in the room below Betty's bedroom in Act 1. It has the effect of God trying to break into the scene. A similar device in Act 2 has Elizabeth audible upstairs, singing to the children. It is a comforting image. The last, of course, is the drum roll heralding the coming execution of Proctor and Rebecca. The drum roll 'crashes' and 'drums rattle like bones'. This, mixed with Hale's hysterical praying, is intended to really send the shudders through the audience.

Language

It is a simple device, but Miller has written quite a few 1692 'archaisms' and turns of phrase to make the dialogue sound authentic to a modern audience.

The use of the expression 'Goody' (short for 'Goodwife') to indicate a married woman is an obvious example, as is the word 'poppet'.

When Danforth says: 'Postponement now speaks a floundering on my part', his use of the word 'speaks' is archaic, old fashioned.

At the end, Elizabeth's 'He have his goodness now' uses 'have' where we would use 'has'. Virtually every line contains examples like this.

Miller's purpose, as well as authenticity, is to have his audience feel the distance in time between themselves and the people of Salem 1692. The audience is alienated by this language.

See below, LANGUAGE ANALYSIS for more detail on this.

LANGUAGE ANALYSIS

Playwrights seek to develop a separate and distinct 'voice' for each character in the play. This gives them their individuality and makes their experiences realistic and able to convey the ideas of the playwright.

Tituba

Because she comes from Barbados, Tituba's language is quite different from the other characters in the play. 'No, no, chicken blood. I give she chicken blood!', ''He say Mr Parris must be kill!' and 'I don't truck with no devil!' are examples. Her experiences back in Barbados lead her to play a role in the 'witchcraft' or magic but it also separates her.

Reverend Hale

Hale's status and expertise is reflected in his language in Act 1. Note how he refers to the devil as 'The Old Boy' (p 40) indicating his familiarity with the devil and that he is not afraid of him.

When he says 'The devil is precise; the marks of his presence are definite as stone' (p 41) he is displaying his expertise. These are indicators of the devil that he is familiar with while others are not. In Act 2 he says to Proctor: 'Theology, sir, is a fortress; no crack in a fortress may be accounted small.' (p 65) This pronouncement is in response to the fact that Proctor could not remember one of the ten commandments (Thou shalt not commit adultery.) His language here reflects his confidence in his role in what is happening.

In Acts 3 and 4, his confidence in what the court is doing unravels and his language becomes anxious, even hysterical. 'You cannot believe them' (p 104), 'Can you not see the blood on my head!!' (p 114) and 'Woman, plead with him!' (p 125) are examples.

Danforth

Deputy Governor Danforth's language reflects his power, status and stubbornness. 'And do you know that near to four hundred are in the jails from Marblehead to Lynn, and upon my signature?'... 'And seventy-two condemned to hang by that signature?' (p 80) This to Francis Nurse, who is trying to defend his wife Rebecca, is all about Danforth's sense of his own power. He is telling Francis that he must be wary because Danforth can put him in gaol or even have him executed, just with his signature.

'But you must understand, sir, that a person is either with this court or he must be counted against it, there be no road between.' (p 85) This is a characteristic argument used throughout history by fear-mongers and extremists. You must be 100% with me or you are 100% against – which in this case means you are with the devil and will be hanged.

Danforth's complete belief in his own infallibility and refusal to budge is seen in his long speech on page 113, including: 'While I speak God's law, I will not crack its voice with whimpering.'

Elizabeth Proctor

By contrast with most of the other characters in the play, Elizabeth's language is mostly plain-spoken and literal. Her language in Act 4 is restrained and undramatic, in a situation of high drama and a matter of literal life and death. 'I am not your judge, I cannot be...Do as you will, do as you will.' (p 120) And finally: 'He have his goodness now. God forbid I take it from him!' (p 126)

The other character in the play whose language is mostly plain and straight-forward is **Rebecca Nurse**.

Archaic language

This means old-fashioned language use. 'Goody' for 'Mrs', 'poppet' for 'rag doll' and 'trafficked' for 'interacted with' are examples, as are all those 'old-fashioned' forms, such as 'there be no road between' and 'I never thought you but a good man.' There are examples of this on every page.

Miller uses these deliberately to alienate the modern audience. As we sit and watch the play, we feel the fact that this is not our era. The way the characters express themselves highlights this.

This enables us to experience the play as 'outsiders' and yet comprehend the experiences the characters are undergoing and apply them to the modern world and our own lives. We don't belong in Salem, it is not our experience. But if the audience notes the similarities to other historical eras, we might think that the warning of Salem applies to our own context.

Metaphorical Language

In *The Crucible*, Miller's characters use an unusual, or you might say unnatural, quantity of metaphorical language. Again, there are examples on every page and all characters do it.

> Parris: 'And I pray you feel the weight of truth upon you...' (p 20)
>
> Abigail: 'I have seen some reddish work done at night'. (p 27)
>
> Abigail: 'and sweated like a stallion whenever I come near!' (p 29)
>
> Francis Nurse: 'My wife is the very brick and mortar of the church, Mr Hale.' (p 67)
>
> Proctor: 'I will fall like an ocean on that court!' (p 72)
>
> Danforth: 'We burn a hot fire here, it melts down all concealment' (p 81)
>
> Proctor: 'She thinks to dance with me on my wife's grave.' (p 98)
>
> Proctor: 'I have made a bell of my honour! I have rung the doom of my good name.' (p 98)
>
> Hale: 'Can you not see the blood on my head!!' (p 114)

These are just a few examples.

Miller uses this metaphorical language in order that the melodrama of the play is heightened. There is a sense of events being at once symbolic as well as literal. This tendency to metaphorical overstatement is one aspect of 'belonging' that is maintained in Salem, to the very end of the play. (Danforth: 'Who weeps for these, weeps for corruption!')

Miller also achieves an effect in the 'ear' of the modern audience of making the dialogue sound biblical.

THE ESSAY

The essay consists of the basic form of an introduction, body paragraphs and conclusion. The esssay has been the subject of numerous texts and you should have the basic form well in hand. As teachers, the point we would emphasise would be to link the paragraphs both to each other and back to your argument (which should directly respond to the question). Of course, ensure your argument is logical and sustained.

Make sure you use specific examples and that your quotes are accurate. To ensure that you respond to the question, make sure you plan carefully and are sure what relevant point each paragraph is making. It is solid technique to actually 'tie up' each point by explicitly coming back to the question.

When composing an essay the basic conventions of the form are:

- State your argument, outline the points to be addressed and perhaps have a brief definition.

↓

A solid structure for each paragraph is:

- Topic sentence (*the main idea and its link to the previous paragraph/ argument*)
- Explanation/ discussion of the point including links between texts if applicable.
- Detailed evidence (*Close textual reference - quotes, incidents and technique discussion.*)
- Tie up by restating the point's relevance to argument/ question

↓

- Summary of points
- Final sentence that restates your argument

As well as this basic structure, you will need to focus on:

Audience – for the essay the audience must be considered formal unless specifically stated otherwise. Therefore, your language must reflect the audience. This gives you the opportunity to use the jargon and vocabulary that you have learnt in English. For the audience ensure your introduction is clear and has impact. Avoid slang or colloquial language including contractions (like 'doesn't', 'e.g.', 'etc.').

Purpose – the purpose of the essay is to answer the question given. The examiner evaluates how well you can make an argument and understand the module's issues and its text(s). An essay is solidly structured so its composer can analyse ideas. This is where you earn marks. It does not retell the story or state the obvious.

Communication – Take a few minutes to plan the essay. If you rush into your answer it is almost certain you will not make the most of the brief 40 minutes to show all you know about the question. More likely you will include irrelevant details that do not gain you marks but waste your precious time. Remember an essay is formal so **do not** do the following: story-tell, list and number points, misquote, use slang or colloquial language, be vague, use non-sentences or fail to address the question.

PLAN:

Don't even think about starting without one!

Introduce...

the texts you are using in the response

Argument: The human experience is affected by:

- Idea One
- Idea Two
- Idea Three

You need to let the marker know what texts you are discussing. You can start with a definition but it can come in the first paragraph of the body. You MUST state your argument in response to the question and the points you will cover as part of it. Wait until the end of the response to give it!

↓

Idea One – Aspect of human experience as outlined in the textual material, e.g. physical impact.

Idea Two – Another aspect of human experience as outlined in the textual material, e.g. psychological impact.

- explain the idea
- where and how is it shown in the prescribed text?
- where and how is it shown in related text 1?

Idea Three – People's sense of experience is affected by context and environment

- explain the idea
- where and how shown in the prescribed text?
- where and how shown in related text 1?

You can use the things you have learned to organise the essay. For each one, you say where you saw this in your prescribed text and where in related text(s).

Two or three ideas are usually enough as you can explore them in detail.

↓

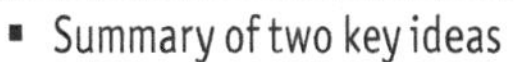

- Summary of two key ideas
- Final sentence that restates your argument

Make sure your conclusion restates your argument. It does not have to be too long.

MODEL ESSAY OUTLINE

To what extent are human experiences significant in the set text?

From your studies respond to this question using your set text and at ONE piece of other textual material

This essay needs to be attacked in a manner that responds to the question and shows ALL your knowledge about the text. The question lends itself to a close study of Arthur Miller's *The Crucible* as the text does show how the human experience is integral to life and how it shapes our other experiences and interaction with the world.

An introduction might be written:

> Human experiences are important in Miller's play *The Crucible* and the two related texts Lawrence's film *Jindabyne* and Ed Sheeran's song *Castle on the Hill*. These texts show how human experiences are integral to human existence and bring more meaning to one's life. Life is about experiences that challenge us and define how we see the world. They shape our beliefs and attitudes and can be confronting at the same time. Without experiences our lives would be empty and meaningless.

Your essay should then follow the outlined plan and develop these ideas. This gives you the opportunity to link the texts and fully develop each of the ideas.

ANNOTATED RELATED MATERIAL: DIFFERENT STUDIES OF HUMAN EXPERIENCES

Jindabyne – Ray Lawrence

Jindabyne is an Australian film that captures a wide array of human experiences. It touches on the ideas mentioned in the introduction to this text in a number of detailed instances. We can begin by considering the following before beginning a detailed examination of the narrative.

The collective human experience:

- Aboriginality and the spiritual;
- The Fishermen and their code;
- The reaction of the townsfolk;
- Media response;
- Interaction with the natural world.

Individual Experience:

- An individual character's response to the body – choose one;
- The killer;
- Response to the revelations;
- Past experiences and how they impact on current experiences;
- Reaction to loss – emotional;
- Assumptions about life.

We can now look at the plot to help us understand each of these issues. *Jindabyne* begins with the sound of a radio being tuned and the Australian feel of the movie is immediate with the theme music for the ABC news. Lawrence emphasises the isolation by having the radio not tune in correctly for an unknown female character, forcing her to use the cassette player. With this unusual beginning we know that her experience is not going to be positive.

We then pan to the rocks slowly where Gregory, our killer, sits patiently in a truck with the engine running watching the road. We know he is prepared for this as he has binoculars. He sees an Aboriginal girl, Susan O'Connor, driving and she is the one fiddling with the radio. He chases her down and forces her to stop. He moves toward her as we see a long shot of how isolated they are. We see his face in her window looming above her and screaming about the electricity coming down from the mountains. This film is no murder mystery, as we know from the beginning that the murderer is Gregory the electrician. This is about the experiences of the other characters in the film and how they respond to current experiences.

The Kane family, Stewart, Claire and son Tom, is waking. Claire pretends to sleep, before waking suddenly and being affectionate with Tom. Stewart and Tom head out fishing. The scene doesn't feel quite right and there is some emotional tension between Stewart and Claire that is unspoken due to what they have experienced in the past. Claire had a complicated past when she was pregnant with Tom. When she finds she is pregnant again, she becomes emotional and slightly unstable.

As the film builds we see the complex pasts of the characters and their interactions in the confinement of the small town. The fishing trip is a break from this and extremely important in their lives.

We see some of the emotional instability in characters such as Caylin-Calandria, who with Tom, has some issues at school. Along with Caylin-Calandria, Claire and Jude also have issues but in a nicely framed shot of the three female characters, we see them conform as members of a close knit group. The sacrifice they make is similar to Gregory's but on a different scale. Note the connection here and how each one is to get back to order and societal norms. This is the collective experience for all the characters.

At the Kanes' home the tensions are obvious from their past experiences but they contain it for appearances' sake. Occasionally, the tension reaches breaking point and the experience strains the superficial approach. The tension builds at home and the fishing trip seems like a good opportunity to break the cycle.

When we see Gregory dump Susan O'Connor's body in the river, we know that the fishing and her death will interact.

The next morning, the fishermen head off for their one big trip of the year and the sign 'Gone fishing' is put in the garage window. We see Billy on the phone to Elissa and putting the sign the wrong way round in the window shows his immaturity. They have already said they are taking him away to make a man of him. The four men have a few beers on the way and talk as they travel through the landscape. They intend to give Billy the experience they think he needs as a 'man' — a cultural rite of passage.

The men arrive and the high-tension electricity wires punctuate the wilderness. They begin to hike toward the valley. It's a long walk in and the terrain is hilly and difficult. They stop on the way and again we see Billy's naivety when Stewart says 'Listen to that' meaning the silence but he can't, as he has his earphones in. It is part of the break in tension of the film that they commune with nature. This experiential break affects all the men. The episode represents a distinct human experience.

Stewart wanders down the river fishing and sees Susan's body caught in the rocks. Hesitantly, he wades out to it and turns it over saying 'Oh Jesus' repeatedly. He screams for the others to come as he drags the body to the bank. He is obviously upset, making the sign of the cross. Stewart tells Rocco to 'take her, for fuck's sake, take her' and their shock is obvious. They all stare at the body and Billy goes to run off but they stop him. The four men meet and decide to leave her in the water and tie her so she doesn't float away.

The presence of the body threatens to detract from the enjoyment of the fishing experience. The act of attempted isolation of the bad experience is expected to evoke only a mild response. They do not anticipate the stormy reaction it receives when they return to the community.

The men go on fishing, with Stewart getting the first big fish on an absolutely perfect day. The lure of the fish is strong, especially when they see the big one he has caught. They have a successful and enjoyable time, a positive experience. They get a photo of the catch and Billy holds up his fish in a typical hunter/gatherer pose. Capturing an experience this way is most enjoyable.

It is a photo that will come back to haunt them as things change back in the world. An unanticipated adverse reaction can be a horrific experience.

Stewart goes to check on the dead girl, rolling her over and getting debris off her face in a quite tender gesture. The next day they head back and report it. At the car Billy rings Elissa and says they found a body but 'caught the most amazing fish'. They are told by the police to wait and seem despondent their trip has been ruined. They organise their story as Stewart says they have 'to get their story straight'.

We cut to Gregory eating breakfast and he appears to be a normal, lonely man until he goes out to his shed where he has hidden Susan's car and this reminds us of the evil in him. Consider his experience and his motivations. How does he see his actions and the world?

The next day at the station the policeman tells the fishermen 'we don't step over bodies for our recreational pursuits' and 'the whole town's ashamed of you'. When they are told to 'piss off' from the station the press are waiting for them and Billy makes a comment. Carl is angry with the press but we can begin to see signs of distress within the whole group.

The experience they had so looked forward to has become a negative one and the tensions we saw before are exacerbated by the emotional and collective response to the murder. Claire soon becomes obsessed with the whole affair because of her own state. The newspaper the next day has the headline, 'Men fish over dead body' because Billy has talked. Billy is late to work and Stewart tells him they have to 'stick together on this'.

Susan's sister calls them 'animals' and raises the race question by asking if they would have left a white girl. The Aboriginal youths begin to attack and vandalise the property of the men in violent outbursts, including throwing a rock through Billy's van window and thus endangering his baby. They insult Carl at the caravan park and vandalise the garage.

The police aren't any help and the situation deteriorates. Jude tells the police they shouldn't be enforcing the 'political correctness' laws. The intervention of the sense of Aboriginality and race challenges the assumptions people have and how we see the world. The contrasting views are ingrained in the social structures and part of different collective experiences.

The Aboriginal people see the white people as 'interfering' and the group of fishermen begin to fight amongst themselves. Elissa says they shouldn't go to the bush at all as it's sacred. The group talk about the bush and Rocco punches Stewart for saying the Aborigines are superstitious. The experience of racial tension becomes ever-present and adds to the emotional responses to the experience.

We now head slowly to a resolution of the conflict brought about by the various experiences. Each is handled in a different manner by characters and you can explore one or two of the responses. To cycle back to the original murder, Claire is stalked by Gregory in his truck. He stops her but drives off after staring weirdly, an odd experience in itself.

Terry and Stewart talk and Stewart meets Rocco and Carl. He tells them Claire's left him 'again'. Rocco can't believe it and we cross cut to her looking out into the wilderness after he looks thoughtfully out the window. These different reactions to experiences mirror attitudes in life and reactions to emotional and intellectual conflict.

In conclusion, Lawrence takes us back to the healing power of nature in our human experiences when the Aboriginal people are having a ceremony. Gregory watches while Claire walks in. Again we see his truck as an omnipresent force in the film, almost an extension of him. An Aboriginal man tells Claire to 'piss off' from the ceremony after she says she has come to pay her 'respects' but he is told to leave her alone by an Auntie.

The smoke and tribal music symbolise the ceremonial nature of the setting and the camera pans around the scene and the bush. We see parts of the ceremony with chanting and clapping sticks. The camera moves in and out while other shots pan around the bush, giving us the full experience and Lawrence portrays this as a positive, healing experience.

Eventually Stewart, Tom, Carl, Jude and Rocco arrive to pay respects. Tom runs to his mother and Stewart goes over and says 'Sorry' but is rebuffed by the father who throws dirt on him and spits, refusing his apology. Then an Aboriginal girl tells a little about Susan's story and sings the last love song Susan wrote.

The camera pans around all the faces as they listen to the song and the ceremonial smoke wafts around. It seems to have some healing effect on everyone, as it is a meaningful experience which raises the idea of the spiritual experience in the text. The girl stops singing through emotion. 'Be gone' seems to symbolise in language the whole scenario for each character.

We see a long wide shot of the bush before fading back to Gregory waiting again in his car behind the rocks for another victim. It is quite a circular conclusion and it is an odd end when he crushes the fly. We don't quite know what to make of the whole experience and he seems to be the only character unchanged by the experiences in the film.

Poem: 'Inland' by John Kinsella

The poem captures the mood and ethos of the outback farming communities and deals with the human aspect more than some of the other poems in Kinsella's collection: *Peripheral Light*. This poem is one long restless thought that mimics memories and recollection while raising the current, topical issues that concern the poet. As usual with his poems Kinsella orientates the audience early with the word 'Inland' and then continues the poem without a full stop. The poem flows with the use of commas but Kinsella allows us to stop and think with the use of the colon, brackets and the hyphen. Look for these punctuation stops as you read as they emphasise a specific point or idea that resonates with the audience.

The first stanza gives us a foreshadowing of the events to follow with the warnings in the words 'storm', 'alert' and 'uncertain'. This ominous tone is reinforced by the word 'ghosts' and the implication of death which is constant in much of Kinsella's poetry. The next stanza deals with a more human element and we get the country feel with the bracketed gossip about McHenry's accident which shows the close knit community. Habits here are formed as part of survival and known to all as we see 'the old man plying the same track' and the families possibly heading to church on the Sunday morning.

The third stanza returns to the vagaries of nature. Kinsella repeats 'uncertain' with regard to the weather. Weather and the environment play a large role in farming communities and it is especially so at sowing and harvest. Despite the uncertainty and 'ashen' days which alter 'moods', the community returns to their habits and routines which shape their lives. The next stage returns to the road and the implication of a journey but a journey that is straight and in conflict with the cycles of the natural world. The path seems already marked and measured. It is 'straight and narrow', marked by a theodolite.

The final four lines of the poem are pure Kinsella, marking the transience of humanity on the landscape. We read

> 'it's a place of borrowed dreams
> where the marks of the spirit
> have been erased by dust –
> the restless topsoil'

The European farmers had 'borrowed dreams' for their own relationship with the land but this line also harks back to the indigenous Dreamtime when the land was created. The indigenous view that the land owns the people is also true for Kinsella. This sense of nobody owning the land is strong in his poetry. European impact on the land can be seen in the spirituality being removed by the dust—dust created by the poor farming techniques transferred from a different land. He finishes with the 'restless topsoil' as if the whole earth is moving in its own discontented journey, just as the people move.

The influence here of genuinely lost spirituality and connection with the land as we move directly on the 'high road' contrasts with the more flowing, 'restless' side of the natural world. This visual contrast is obvious but we can also discuss the contrast between habit and spirit. 'Inland' is a poem that uses the landscape to show the contrast between two views of the countryside.

DRAMA: Eugene O'Neil's *Desire Under the Elms*

O'Neill sets out to instruct how the house and elms should appear and the year is 1850. Note how he describes the 'enormous' elms as,

> 'exhausted women resting their sagging breasts and hands and hair on its roof, and when it rains their tears trickle down monotonously and rot on the shingles'

and how they dominate and 'rot'. It is important to read this both in terms of the play and in the context of American theatre. The description here shows O'Neill's genius at new design and original theatricality.

Part One: Scene One

The whole first page and a third are nearly all playwright notes that describe the farm, the house and the characters of Eben, Simeon and Peter. The first words of the play, 'God! Purty!' reflect the beauty of the land and how Eben perceives it. Eben is 'resentful and defensive' and feels 'trapped' on the farm.

His older half-brothers Simeon and Peter are 'more bounce and homelier in face, shrewder and more practical.' They all have worked hard on their father's farm over the years and have little feeling for their absent father. We learn that Simeon had a 'woman' who died and that Peter is excited by the prospect of 'gold in the West'. They all talk about how hard they've worked and hope that the father might 'die soon'. What we get from all this is that they are earthy and this is reflected in their bodies and clothes which are all dirt stained.

We also see here the difference between them as Eben sees gold in the pasture, not California, as they head in for a dinner of bacon in what seems a ritual they have performed many times before. Note that O'Neill calls for the use of the curtain at the end of the scene.

Scene Two

It is twilight and again we get detailed notes on the interior scene. Simeon tells Eben he should not wish their father dead and Eben replies he's not his son but, 'I'm Maw – every drop of blood!' He then blames the father, Ephraim Cabot, for killing his mother by working her to death but the others just say there was work to be done. O'Neill gets them to list the jobs and Eben comes back with 'vengeful passion' that, while they did nothing, he will see his mother gets 'rest and sleep in her grave!'

They then discuss Cabot's absence and how he just drove off in a buggy one day in a rush. Simeon says that when he went,

> 'He druv off in the buggy, all spick an' span, with the mare all breshed an' shiny, druv off clackin' his tongue an' wavin' his whip. I remember it quite well'

Eben mocks Simeon for not stopping him and the scene concludes with Eben leaving to see Minnie the town whore. We learn all the Cabot men have slept with her. Simeon and Peter say that Eben is just like 'Paw' and thinks of California. The final image is of Eben with his arms stretched to the sky talking about starts and sin, 'my sin's as purty as any one on 'em!', until he 'strides' to the village for Min.

Scene Three

It is 'pitch darkness' and Eben comes home with the news that Cabot has married a 'purty' thirty-five year old. He has heard this in the village and this effectively disinherits the boys. Simeon and Peter see California as their only option now. Eben tells the boys that they can have three hundred dollars each if they sign their share of the farm over to him. He can get the money as his mother told him,

> 'I know whar it's hid. I been waitin' – Maw told me. She knew whar it lay fur years, but she was waitin'....It's her'n – the money he hoarded from her farm an' hid from Maw. It's my money by rights now.'

They think about it and Eben tells them about his night with Min. He tells how he hates the new wife after the boys suggest he might sleep with her, just like Min, to get the old man back. Peter and Simeon say they'll do the deal and leave the farm. Both are bitter and vindictive about Cabot.

Scene Four

The setting is the same as Scene Two and the boys are discussing how they don't have to work now – it is all down to Eben who is jubilant as he thinks it will all be his. Peter and Simeon again reflect on how like his father he is, 'Like his Paw'. They also tell he isn't much of a milker but they soon talk about their leaving and how they'll miss some aspects of the farm.

Eben comes back in and says that the 'old mule an the bride' are coming. The two older boys begin to pack and sign Eben's papers as he gives them the money Cabot had hidden. They tell him they'll send him 'a lump o' gold for Christmas' and head into the yard feeling 'light' because of their newfound freedom.

Ephraim Cabot and Abbie Putnam then come in and O'Neill describes them in detail. Cabot is

> 'seventy-five, tall and gaunt, with great, wiry, concentrated power, but stoop shouldered by toil. His face is hard as if it were hewn from a boulder, yet there is a weakness in it'

but his face is weakened with petty pride. Abbie is

> 'thirty-five, buxom, full of vitality. Her round face is pretty but marred by its rather gross sensuality. There is strength and obstinacy in her jaw, a hard determination in her eyes, and about her whole personality.'

She also has a 'desperate quality'. Cabot shows Abbie the place and she says to him it's 'mine'. Then he sees the two boys not working. He introduces Abbie and she goes to look at 'her' house and they warn her Eben's inside.

Cabot tells them to get to work and they give him cheek, saying they are 'free' and heading to California. They 'whoop' it up and he says he'll have them chained up. They throw rocks at the house, smashing the window and head off singing. Abbie sticks her head out the window and says she likes the room but he is thinking of the stock and 'almost runs' to the barn.

Abbie then meets Eben in the kitchen and talks to him in 'seductive tones'. She says she doesn't want to be his 'Maw' but friends and he cusses her. She tells him of her troubled life and how Cabot gave her a chance to escape it. He calls her a 'harlot' and they argue over ownership of the farm. She has the upper hand in law and he leaves but the seeds of their growing attraction have been set.

Outside he and his father argue about life and work and he tells Eben 'Ye'll never be more'n half a man!' The scene ends with Abbie washing up and the faint notes of the song the boys were singing as they left.

Part Two: Scene One

Again O'Neill describes in detail the farmhouse setting. Two months have passed and it is a hot Sunday afternoon. Abbie in her best outfit is sitting on the porch and Eben comes out of the house also dressed in his best. They stalk each other, both attracted and repelled. As he walks away she 'gives a sneering, taunting chuckle' at him and they argue but the attraction is obvious. She says that nature will pull him to her but he says that she is married and he goes to leave her.

She accuses him of going to Min and she gets angry stating he'll never get the farm,

> 'Ye'll never live t' see the day when even a stinkin' weed on it 'll belong t' ye!'

He says he hates her and leaves as Cabot enters. She tells him Eben has been mocking him and twists the conversation to the inheritance of the farm. She tells him Eben lusts after her and as he angers she backs off in her accusations. Reassured, he says that she can have the farm if she bears the son she says she wants with him. He says that he'd 'do anythin' ye axed, I tell ye!' if she gave him a son and tells her to pray to God for it to happen.

Scene Two

It is about eight in the evening and here the bedrooms are highlighted, with Eben in one and Cabot with Abbie in the other. The two of them are talking about a son. They seem together, yet apart, as he tells her of his life on the farm and how God's hard. He both lost and gained on the way through, but the farm is his. He says he is pleased he found her, his 'Rose o' Sharon'. Abbie promises him that she will bear a son as he basically threatens her,

> 'Ye don't know nothin' – nor never will. If ye don't hev a son t' redeem ye...'

and he leaves to sleep in the barn with the cows 'whar it's restful'.

We then see Eben and Abbie restless and she leaves the room and goes to him. He 'submits' to her kisses then 'hurls' her away. Abbie says she'd make him 'happy' and she knows he wants her too much. She tells him to go down to the parlour and he is shocked as this is where his mother was 'laid out'. She leaves for the parlour and he wonders what's happening. The scene closes with a question to his dead mother, 'Maw! Whar are yew?' but we know that he wants her and will go to her.

Scene Three

The scene now shifts to the parlour which is described as a 'grim, repressed room like a tomb'. Abbie waits and Eben appears and he sits at her invitation. They talk about his Maw and how they hate Cabot. Abbie throws herself at him with 'wild passion' and he is caught up in the moment and thinks that it's his Maw wanting him to sleep with Abbie to get revenge on Cabot,

> I see it! I sees why. It's her vengeance on him – so's she kin rest quiet in her grave!

Abbie proclaims her love for him and he for her then they kiss 'in a fierce, bruising kiss' to close the scene.

Scene Four

A more bold and confident Eben leaves the house and Abbie opens the parlour window. She calls him over for a kiss and they talk a bit before Eben says his Maw can now rest. They split as Cabot comes out of the barn but are now obviously in love. Eben tells Cabot that his Maw is now at rest and Cabot says he rests best with the cows. Cabot is confused but the scene ends with him criticising Eben as 'Soft-headed' and a 'born fool' but, being a practical man, he heads for breakfast.

Part Three: Scene One

Time has passed to 'late spring the following year'. Eben is upstairs in emotional and psychological conflict while a party happens downstairs. Cabot has drunk too much and Abbie sits, pale and thin, in a rocking chair. There is a fiddler and Abbie begins the scene by asking for Eben and the guests 'titter' as most think the baby is Eben's, not Cabot's, which is true enough. They laugh and Cabot is angered by this and orders them to dance. The fiddler 'slyly' says they're waiting for Eben but Cabot mocks the boy and then ensues a bawdy conversation about his fertility,

> I got a lot in me – a hell of a lot – folks don't know on. Fiddle 'er up, durn ye! Give 'em somethin' t' dance t!'

The fiddler plays and they dance. Cabot joins in frantically and 'whoop(s)' it up. He exhausts the fiddler and pours whiskey. In the upstairs room Eben is looking at the baby. Abbie goes upstairs and Cabot leaves for outside, 'fresh air', as she has told him not to 'tech' her. The guests gossip after he goes and we see Eben and Abbie upstairs and she professes her love for him,

> 'Don't git feelin' low. I love ye, Eben. Kiss me.'

Cabot says he's going to rest in the barn. The scene concludes with the fiddler playing in celebration of 'the old skunk gittin' fooled!'

Scene Two

Eben is outside half an hour later and Cabot is coming back from the barn. Cabot tells him to get a woman inside and he might get a farm. Eben replies that this farm's his and Cabot mocks him. He tells her Abbie has been promised the farm for her son and Eben is angered thinking Abbie has tricked him.

Eben goes to kill her but Cabot is too strong for him and Abbie comes out to stop him choking Eben. Cabot tells him he's weak and goes inside to celebrate. Abbie tries to be tender with Eben but he rejects her and calls her a liar.

> 'Ye're nothin' but a stinkin' passel o' lies. Ye've been lyin' t' me every word ye spoke, day an' night, since we fust – done it. Ye've kept sayin' ye loved me....'

She says she loves him and tells him that the promise was made before they fell in love. He says he'll go to California.

They argue and he 'torturedly' says he wished the baby had never been born. Abbie is distraught and she says she'd kill the baby to prove her love for him. He says he won't listen to her but she calls after him that she can 'prove' she loves him and she 'kin do one thin' God does'. Abbie is desperate at the end of the scene.

Scene Three

It is now just before dawn and Eben is in the kitchen ready to leave. Abbie is near the cradle with 'her face full of terror'. She sobs but Cabot stirs and she goes to the kitchen and flings her arms around Eben, kissing him 'wildly'. She says 'I killed him' and he thinks she means Cabot but is horrified when she tells him it's the baby.

Eben states it was his baby and she says she loved it but loves him more. He is angered,

> 'Don't ye tech me! Ye're pizzen! How could ye – t' murder
> a pore little critter – Ye must've swapped yer soul t' hell!

and tells her that he is getting the Sheriff and heads, 'panting and sobbing' to town. She calls out to him that she loves him.

Scene Four

It is after dawn and Abbie is in the kitchen. Cabot wakes in his room and is concerned that he has woken late. He checks the baby and is proud it is quiet and asleep. He goes down to Abbie in the kitchen and she tells him the baby is dead. He runs to check and comes back down and asks 'why?'

In a rage she tells him it was Eben's son and that she loves Eben, not him. He blinks back a tear and then gets 'stony' so he can carry on and says he is going to get the Sheriff. Abbie tells him that Eben's already gone so that Cabot tells her he'll 'git t' wuk.' He then tells her he'd never have told and now he's going to be 'lonesomer'n ever!' Eben comes back and Cabot tells him to get off the farm.

Eben asks for her forgiveness and tells her he loves her. He says he realised he loved her at the Sheriff's and they have a chance to run away but Abbie says she'll take her punishment. Eben says he will share it with her and plans to tell the Sheriff they planned it together. They think they can stand it together and then Cabot comes back.

He goes into a long tirade and tells them how he's let the stock go and will burn the house down. He too plans to go to California but finds that Eben has gotten to his money first. Cabot says that this is a sign from God to him to stay and that 'God's hard an' lonesome!' At this point the Sheriff comes and Eben says he was involved with the baby's murder.

Cabot says 'Take 'em both' and leaves to get his stock. The sun is coming up and as they are led away Eben says the farm's 'Purty' and Abbie agrees. The Sheriff finishes the play with the line, 'It's a jim-dandy farm, no denyin'. Wish I owned it!'

OTHER RELATED TEXTS

Fiction / Non-fiction / Drama

- *Wonder* – R G Palacio
- *First they Killed My Father* – Luong Ung
- *The Graveyard Book* – Neil Gaiman
- *Looking for Alaska* – John Green
- *Eleanor and Park* by Rainbow Rowell
- *The Fault in Our Stars* – John Green
- *We All Fall Down* – Robert Cormier
- *The Old Man and the Sea* – Ernest Hemingway
- *The Fire Eaters* – David Almond
- *Ender's Game* – Orson Scott Card
- *Hatchet* – Gary Paulsen
- *Inside Black Australia* – Kevin Gilbert
- *Sapiens: A Brief History of Humankind* – Yuval Noah Harari
- *Peeling the Onion* – Wendy Orr
- *Raw* – Scott Monk
- *Six Degrees of Separation* – John Guare
- *The Book Thief* – Markus Zusak
- *When Dogs Cry* – Markus Zusak
- *Holes* – Louis Sachar
- *The Outsiders* – S.E. Hinton
- *Roll of Thunder, Hear My Cry* – Mildred D. Taylor
- *A Small Free Kiss in the Dark* – Glenda Millard
- *Monster* – Walter Dean Myers
- *Lord of the Flies* – William Golding
- *Jandamarra* – Steve Hawke
- *A Separate Peace* – John Knowles
- *A Monster Calls* – Patrick Ness
- *The Pigman* – Paul Zindel
- *The Invention of Hugo Cabret* – Brian Selznik

- *Emerald City* – David Williamson
- *Silent Spring* – Rachel Carson

Films and Television

- *The Human Experience* – Charles Kinnane
- *My Brilliant Career* – Gillian Armstrong
- *Broadchurch* – James Strong & Euros Lyn
- *Twinsters* – Samantha Futerman and Ryan Miyamoto
- *Be My Brother* – Genevieve Clay - Smith
- *What's Eating Gilbert Grape* – Lasse Hallstrom
- *Pleasantville* – Gary Ross
- *Eternal Sunshine of the Spotless Mind* – Michel Gondry
- *Taxi Driver* – Martin Scorsese
- *Tootsie* – Sydney Pollack
- *Back in Time for Dinner* – Kim Maddever
- *The Godfather* – Francis Ford Coppola
- *Friends* – David Crane and Marta Kaufmann
- *Dawson's Creek* – Kevin Williamson
- *Orange is the New Black* – Jenji Kohan
- *Boy Meets World* – Michael Jacobs and April Kelly

Website – quote on literature and the human experience

http://view2.fdu.edu/academics/university-college/school-of-humanities/english-language-and-literature-program/

> At its most fundamental level literature explores what it means to be a human being in this world and tries to describe what our human experience is like. As such, literature pushes us to confront the large human questions that have plagued humankind for centuries: issues of fate and free will, issues relating to our role in the universe, our relationship to God, and our

relationships with others. Studying literature not only helps us to understand the complexity of these questions intellectually, but because of its very nature, it allows us to experience these tensions vicariously. Literature does not just tell us about human experience; it recreates it in a way we can feel and visualise. In other words, it calls for a total response from us—it stretches us beyond who we are.

First, literature can enhance our ability to relate to people. Because literature focuses on human relationships and self perception, it can broaden our own experience—to help us understand different kinds of people, different cultures, different problems—and, consequently, help us better understand our own relationships with others.

The study of literature also helps to foster an appreciation for beauty, symmetry, and order. This means more than the intuitive response of liking or disliking something we see or read or hear; it means a carefully thought-through response that will enhance appreciation—not destroy it.

Perhaps the most important skills that the study of literature teaches are analytic and synthetic skills. In learning to read carefully and analytically, we learn to ask hard questions both of the work and of ourselves. And as we seek to discover the relationships between the ideas and images we uncover in a work, our ultimate goal is to see the whole—to see how the parts work together to make the piece what it is. In grappling with the complex and difficult ideas contained in literature, we learn to accept the multiple dimensions and ambiguity that are so often present in life.

Finally, the study of literature will also help develop our writing abilities as we come to value the written word and understand its power to communicate.

Beyond all of these skills, however, it is not what literature can do for us as individuals as much as what it can do to us. Literature speaks to the whole person. Listen to it, says C. S. Lewis, and you will be changed.

Poetry

- 'Warren Pryor' – Alden Nowlan
- 'The Gardener' – Louis MacNeice
- 'The Improvers' – Colin Thiele

Songs

- *Be My Escape* – Relient K
- *Mandolin Wind* – Rod Stewart
- *Roxanne* – The Police
- *Wake Me Up When September Ends* – Green Day
- *Under Pressure* – Queen & David Bowie
- *Candle in the Wind* – Elton John
- *Empire State of Mind* – Alicia Keys
- *Gold Digger* – Kanye West
- *We Are Young* – Fun.
- *Centrefold* – J. Geils Band
- *It's Time* – Imagine Dragons
- *We Cry* – The Script
- *If I Were a Boy* – Beyoncé
- *Shake it Out* – Florence + the Machine
- *C'mon* – Panic! At the Disco & Fun.
- *I Don't Love You* – My Chemical Romance
- *Sing* – My Chemical Romance
- *1985* – Bowling for Soup
- *What About Me* – Shannon Noll
- *Sinner* – Jeremy Loops
- *7 Years* – Lucas Graham

- *Bitter Sweet Symphony* – The Verve
- *Ghost!* – Kid Kudi
- *Good Riddance (Time of Your Life)* – Green Day
- *Expectations* – Belle and Sebastian
- *After Hours* – We Are Scientists
- *Write About Love* – Belle and Sebastian
- *Trust Your Stomach* – Marching Band
- *Heaven Knows I'm Miserable Now* – The Smiths